3rd July 2010

For dear Peter — wishing you a very happy birthday — I know you have a love of organs so I hope this is of some use —
　　with love Loowee & Paul x

The Box of Whistles

*The history and recent development
of organ case design*

John Norman

AZURE

To Jill
Her encouragement, patience and forbearance made this book possible

First published in Great Britain in 2007
Society for Promoting Christian Knowledge
36 Causton Street
London SW1P 4ST

Copyright © John Norman 2007

All rights reserved. No part of this book may be reproduced or transmitted in any form or by any means, electronic or mechanical, including photocopying, recording, or by any information storage and retrieval system, without permission in writing from the publisher.

SPCK does not necessarily endorse the individual views contained in its publications.

British Library Cataloguing-in-Publication Data
A catalogue record for this book is available from the British Library

ISBN 978–1–902694–31–3

1 3 5 7 9 10 8 6 4 2

Typeset by Graphicraft Limited, Hong Kong
Printed in China by New Era Printing Company

CONTENTS

	Introduction	iv
	Acknowledgements	vi
	Further reading	vi
1	What is an organ case?	1
2	Pipes on show	7
3	Gothic and Renaissance origins	14
4	Father Smith and Renatus Harris	23
5	Queen Anne and Georgian	36
6	Back to basics?	57
7	The real Gothic revival	64
8	Not all Gothic	75
9	American showmanship reveals all	83
10	The new brutalism (and after)	86
11	Present-day eclecticism	100
	Index	119

INTRODUCTION

After a dispute with the organbuilder Bernard Smith, Sir Christopher Wren is reputed to have referred to the organ in St Paul's Cathedral as 'that damned box of whistles'. Although the story is now thought to be apocryphal, this book is about the box, not the whistles. It is a celebration of the organ case, its decoration and its many and diverse forms. It covers mainly the organ case in Britain, though reference has to be made to Continental origins because no early British cases survive. But the main reason for this book is the revival in organ case design since 1960, a revival which, so far, has been little documented.

The organ is a wind instrument but, unlike other wind instruments, it has a separate pipe for each note. The pitch of the organ can reach both the upper and lower limits of the human ear. Variety of tone is provided by different sorts of pipes and even a medium-sized instrument may well contain over 1,000 pipes ranging in length from a few inches to 16 feet. For flexibility in playing, the pipes are often grouped in separate departments, each with its own keyboard, so that players can quickly switch from one sound to another. The largest and deepest-toned pipes are usually played with the feet from a pedal keyboard.

The organ dates back to classical antiquity in its invention and more than a thousand years in the service of the church. The organ has a greater variety of sound than any other single instrument. Its flexibility makes it relevant to many different styles of music. The sustained sound provides more support to the human voice than any other instrument. This has remained the basis of its use in churches for many centuries.

A hundred years ago many organbuilders begrudged spending money on organ cases. In 1888 the noted organbuilder 'Father' Henry Willis persuaded the authorities at Truro Cathedral to omit all the upper casework and use the money so saved to provide two extra ranks of pipes inside the instrument. Many players would applaud this decision. After all, the more pipes there are in the organ, the more variety of tone is available, making the instrument more fun to play.

But is this really always true? Perhaps Father Willis was wrong and there is a downside to spending the money on pipes rather than casework. After all, the general public usually place visual considerations before acoustical and musical ones. Too often organs are condemned to out-of-the-way positions because they fail to be an ornament to their surroundings. Money spent on the case can justify a better position for the instrument and thus have a musical value as well as a visual one.

As probably the largest piece of furniture in a building, any organ case has an architectural dimension. Indeed, almost from the earliest times, organ cases have tended to reflect the architectural fashions of the day. Nevertheless, with distinguished exceptions, most organ cases have been designed by organbuilders, not by architects, and this still holds true today. One of the merits of this process is that organbuilder designers tend to take a fairly functional view of the organ case and decorate it as required, rather than bring in extraneous visual ideas. It is surely better to decorate a construction than construct a decoration.

In the interests of clarity and brevity, the design and decoration of chamber organs has been mostly omitted, even though, in the eighteenth century, some very fine pieces were made, including more than one designed by Robert Adam. Also, with a few exceptions, all the organ cases illustrated still exist today and can be studied on site, even though some are a long way away from Britain.

One of the problems of looking at organ cases in Britain today is that, thanks to the destruction wrought by the sixteenth-century iconoclasts, we have only one organ case made before 1600 and precious few made before 1660. Sadly, the splendid and ancient heritage of medieval organ cases found in Continental Europe has no counterpart here. Yet the hundred or so years that followed the restoration of the monarchy in 1660 was one of the finest eras of organ case design in England. After that was a period of relative decline. There was a brief resurgence, confined largely to important instruments, in the last quarter of the nineteenth century, but that was followed by another 60 years of mediocrity. However, in the last 40 years there has been a substantial revival. Today hardly a single organ is built without a case of at least competent design. Perhaps this is a recognition that, long-lived as organs are, organ cases last even longer. Partly, too, it may be a subconscious feeling that if money is being spent on a real organ, not a short-lived electronic imitation, one should be proud of it and make a display of its visual qualities as well as its musical ones.

In the captions, the organbuilder credited with an instrument was the one responsible for the organ at the time the case was made. Since then, the instrument itself may well have been altered or replaced by other hands.

ACKNOWLEDGEMENTS

Thanks are due to Nicholas Thistlethwaite, Nicholas Plumley, Dominic Gwynn and Jim Berrow for reading the text and making suggestions. Nevertheless, the author takes full responsibility for both opinions and mistakes. Thanks are also due to William McVicker, Andrew Hayden, José Hopkins, Frances Moule, Mark Dancer, Chris Knapton, Jim Berrow, John Brennan, the Marquess of Salisbury, the University of York, the Lord Great Chamberlain, Mercatorfonds in Antwerp, the Rijksmuseum in Amsterdam and to various organbuilders for permission to use their photographs or drawings. The author is also grateful to the authorities at colleges in Oxford and Cambridge, King's College, London, numerous city and suburban London churches, Eton College, City of London School, also the cathedrals of Birmingham, Chichester, Clifton, Coventry, Gloucester, Liverpool and Norwich, and Westminster Abbey, as well as the Lady Lever Gallery, Port Sunlight; the National Museum of Wales, Cardiff; the Old Royal Naval College, Greenwich; and the churches of St Bartholomew, Armley, Great St Mary's, Cambridge, and St Peter Mancroft, Norwich, for granting the author photographic access. Nicholas Plumley kindly provided access to his wonderful library of books and prints and Jim Berrow the watercolour of Birmingham Cathedral. Artwork and photographs not otherwise credited are from the author's collection but indulgence is sought if, inadvertently, an illustration has been used without permission.

Finally, a very big debt of thanks is due to the author's father, Herbert Norman, not only for his many drawings but for the inspiration he gave the author to enter the wonderful world of organbuilding, with its wide-ranging artistic and technical challenges.

Further reading

Stephen Bicknell,
The History of the English Organ,
Cambridge University Press (1996).

Joseph E. Blanton, *The Organ in Church Design*,
Venture Press, Albany, Texas (1957).

Cecil Clutton and Austin Niland,
The British Organ, Batsford, London (1963),
2nd edition, Eyre Methuen, London (1982).

Andrew Freeman, *English Organ Cases*,
London (1921).

A. G. Hill, *The Organ-cases and Organs of the Middle Ages and Renaissance*, London (1883 and 1891),
reprinted Frits Knuf, Hilversum (1966).

John Norman, *The Organs of Britain*,
David & Charles, Newton Abbot (1984).

Organ Building, published annually from 2001,
Institute of British Organ Building,
Bury St Edmunds.

The Organbuilder, published annually 1984–2000,
Positif Press, Oxford.

John Rowntree and John Brennan,
The Classical Organ in Britain, Vol. 1: 1955–1974,
Vol. 2: 1975–1978, Vol. 3: 1979–1990,
Positif Press, Oxford.

Nicholas Thistlethwaite, *The Making of the Victorian Organ*,
Cambridge University Press (1990).

1
WHAT IS AN ORGAN CASE?

Roman organ (Hydraulus), c.AD 100, based on a mosaic found at Buk Ammera, Zliten, Libya.

Semi-portable fifteenth-century organ. Panel from a triptych by Jan van Eyck, 1432, in St Bavo's Cathedral, Ghent. (Photo: © Mercatorfonds, Antwerp)

It has to be admitted that, for the first 1,500 years of its existence as a musical instrument, the organ did not have a case in the form we understand it today. The organs known to ancient Rome (did Nero really play the organ?) were quite small, with a single keyboard, a compass of two octaves at most and probably no more than four ranks of pipes. Their appearance was purely functional, with simple panelling to cover the mechanism and a stay to hold the pipes in position.

Knowledge of organ construction, like much of Greek and Roman culture, was lost to the West on the fall of the Roman empire but survived in Byzantium. Although few details exist, we know that it was reintroduced to the West in the eighth century and, before long, was pressed into the service of the Church. We have few records of the instruments of this time, although a tenth-century written account of an organ in Winchester Cathedral suggests that it was bigger than any that the Romans knew.

However, the first reasonably realistic depiction of an organ, by Jan van Eyck in 1432, still shows quite a small, semi-portable instrument of simple un-cased form with modest Gothic ornamentation on the end of the pipe-stay and the front face of the soundboard. One can see that the relation between the position of the keys and that of the pipes was a fairly straightforward one, requiring only the simplest of mechanical connections between the keys and the pallet valves that let the air into the pipes.

The organ case appears to have developed as a result of both practical requirements and mechanical invention. Portable and semi-portable instruments could be locked away in a safe place when not in use, but a larger organ would be too heavy to be moved and needed protection against dust, vermin and vandals. This protection could be achieved by building a wooden box around the pipes with doors on the front which could be opened when the organ was in use. Such a box would look much more elegant if it were symmetrical, but early organs necessarily had their pipes arranged from bass to treble in the same order as the keys. A few bass pipes could be moved to fresh positions, however, with the aid of wind ducts ('conveyances') above or within the soundboard.

Mechanical problems inevitably arose in the design of larger instruments. The spacing of the valves would need to be widened to allow larger pipes, yet the spacing of the keys could not be increased because of the limitations of the human hand span. This was overcome, possibly some time in the fourteenth century, by the invention of the roller. This is a simple mechanical device consisting of a rod rotating between two pivots, with two arms, one connected to the key and one to the pallet valve that lets the air into the corresponding pipe or pipes. The roller makes it possible for the action of the key to be, as it were, transposed sideways, allowing the layout of the pipes to be independent of the layout of the keys. It was but a short step further, with

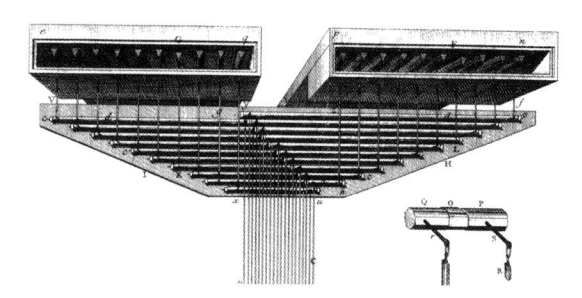

Rollerboard and sample action roller. (Drawing from Dom Bédos de Celles, L'Art du Facteur d'Orgues, *1778)*

Section through a simple organ, showing a waisted case and action rollerboard. (Drawing by Herbert Norman)

2   The Box of Whistles

The earliest surviving playable organ, dating from c.1400, at Notre Dame de Valère, Sion, Switzerland. (Drawing by Herbert Norman)

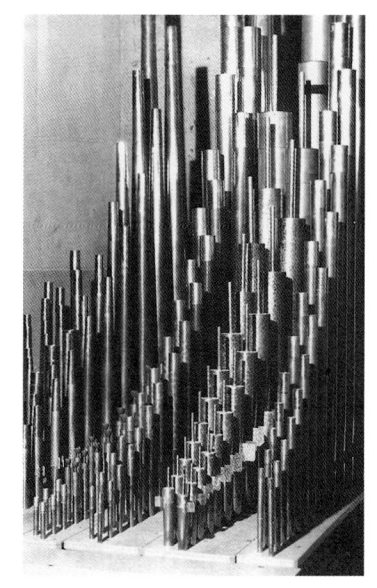

Some of the internal pipes of an organ. (Photo: Hill Norman & Beard)

the aid of a bank of rollers mounted on a 'rollerboard', to rearrange the pipes in a symmetrical layout with alternate notes moved to the other end of the soundboard, opening up important possibilities for the appearance of the organ.

The earliest surviving playable organ, in the Church of Notre Dame de Valère, Sion, Switzerland, dates from about 1400 and has a case of this symmetrical form. The bass pipes are in 'towers' at the ends and the treble pipes in a separate compartment in the middle. The result is an organ whose case has a distinctive silhouette and which can provide the background for considerable architectural decoration.

Note that the case is 'waisted-in' at the bottom. This follows the mechanical construction in that the invention of the rollerboard allowed the pipes to be spread over a greater distance than the width of the keyboard. The result of this is that the case is essentially of a two-box design divided by a support rail known as the 'impost'. The lower section contains the keys, bellows, key action and the mechanism for controlling which ranks of pipes are in use (the 'stop action'). The upper and larger section contains the soundboard (a large flat box on which the pipes stand and which contains the valves which admit air to the pipes in response to movement of the keys and stops). Later organs abandoned the 'waisted-in' construction to allow more room for mechanism. The provision of doors, often closed when the organ was not in use and in Lent, also fell into disuse in later centuries.

Essentially the basic structure of an organ case is that of a large wooden wardrobe. The internal pipes are normally arranged in rows parallel to the front of the case, a layout dictated by the stop-action mechanism. The largest pipes are then placed on show in the front of the case, fed with wind by conveyances from above the soundboard. This can lead to confusion for the lay person who may think that they are the

The interior of an organ.
(Drawing from Dom Bédos de Celles,
L'Art du Facteur d'Orgues, *1778)*

complete instrument. Some years ago, the chief engineer of a not inconsiderable local authority complained about the estimate for cleaning the town hall organ because 'after all, there are only 37 pipes'. Actually there were a couple of thousand.

The overall height of the upper part of the organ case, above the impost, is usually determined by the length of the longest pipe. Thus, in many organs today, the longest pipe in the case will have a nominal length of 8 ft, as this is the length of the lowest note of the Open Diapason stop if the compass of the instrument goes down two octaves below middle C. This nominal length refers to the distance from the top of the pipe down as far as the mouth – the length of the lower tapered portion of the pipe does not affect the pitch of the note. Before 1840, the normal compass of the organ in Britain descended to G, two octaves and a fourth below middle C. This made the longest pipe a nominal 10 ft long – the reason why many eighteenth-century cases are taller than later cases, since the largest pipe, including its foot, is about 12 ft (3.6 m) tall. Many cathedral organ cases have 16 ft front pipes and a few have 32 ft pipes on display, as do some concert-hall instruments.

Sometimes, of course, the space available for the organ prevents the lowest note from standing in the case. Organbuilders tend to avoid this, however, as it means either placing the

4 The Box of Whistles

The mechanism of a double organ. Note: It is no longer usual for players to wear a sword. (Drawing from Dom Bédos de Celles, L'Art du Facteur d'Orgues, 1778)

biggest pipes inside, with consequent space and mechanical complications, or compromising the tone by using either complicated 'Haskell' pipes or 'stopped pipes' (only half as long but with a weaker tone and a different harmonic structure, sometimes augmented with open 'helper' pipes).

The organ has been considered so far as a single 'box of whistles', as one piece of furniture. This is not always so in practice. For flexibility in playing, the pipes are often grouped in separate departments, each with its own keyboard, so that players can quickly switch from one sound to another. When our seventeenth-century forebears wrote of a 'double organ' they meant an organ standing on a gallery with a second and smaller case projecting out from the gallery edge behind the player containing the pipes controlled by the second keyboard. They called this smaller case and its contents the 'Chair' organ to distinguish it from the larger 'Great' organ. This division has stopped pipes for its unison (8 ft) rank, called Stopped Diapason. Not only do they make a different sound but these pipes are only half as long as the corresponding 8 ft Open Diapason in the main case. The Chair case is correspondingly less tall and is said to have a 'four-foot front' (five-foot in the case of a G-compass organ) since the actual case pipes are the bass notes of

The underside (soffit) of a projecting chair case. Christchurch Priory: David Graebe, 1998. (Photo: Nicholson & Co.)

What is an organ case?   5

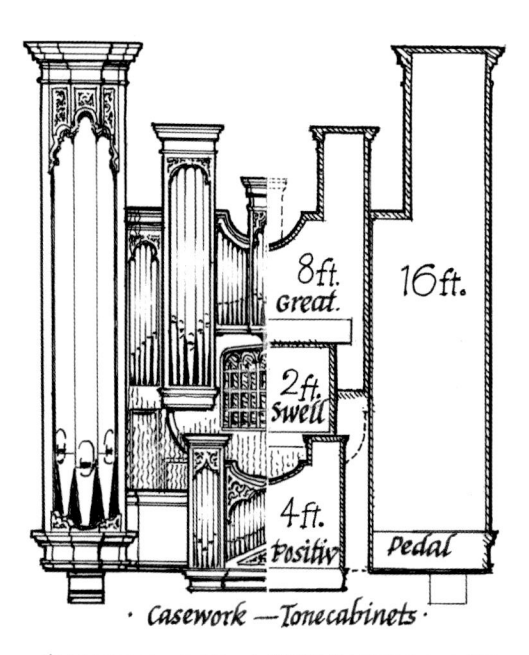

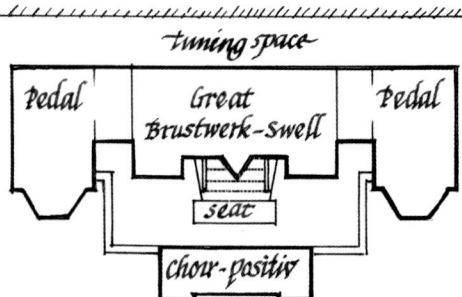

Elevation and plan of an organ arranged according to the Continental Werkprinzip. *The dimensions on the drawing refer to the nominal length of the longest pipe in each department of the instrument.*
(Drawing by Herbert Norman)

the 4 ft Principal rank which speak an octave higher than the Diapasons. Such a layout was at one time very common and although in later years the 'Choir' organ, as it became, was more often incorporated within the main case, many examples of this arrangement remain, especially in our cathedrals and college chapels. The visual contrast between two organ cases of different size can often be very attractive, and is sometimes heightened where the two cases are of different date, which is less uncommon than might be supposed.

On the Continent, the concept of the 'double organ' was carried much further, especially in the magnificent instruments built in Holland and Hanseatic North Germany in the early eighteenth century. These instruments not only had the double organ arrangement with a smaller Chair organ (German *Rückpositiv*) but also had separate casework for the Pedal organ. The British organ had no Pedal organ then, or indeed for another century, but the Hanseatic organ often had two Pedal cases containing pipes speaking alternate notes, placed either side of the *Hauptwerk* (Great organ), sometimes adjoining it and sometimes separate. Larger instruments had a third manual department clearly visible, either an *Oberwerk* above the *Hauptwerk* or a *Brustwerk* below it. This arrangement of an organ, which requires a great deal of height but little depth of floor space, is known as the *Werkprinzip*.

6   The Box of Whistles

2
PIPES ON SHOW

Painted decoration on front pipes from the seventeenth century. Gloucester Cathedral: Thomas Harris, 1665.

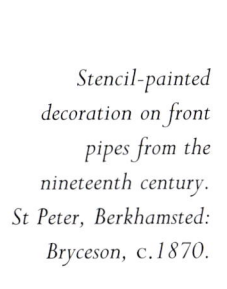

Stencil-painted decoration on front pipes from the nineteenth century. St Peter, Berkhamsted: Bryceson, c.1870.

The 'front pipes' on display are important to the lay person because, even when the instrument is silent, they proclaim the nature of the organ within. However, as noted in the previous chapter, they are not the complete instrument. A few years ago, a building contractor sheeted over the front pipes before starting work on repairing the roof of a Unitarian chapel. After he had removed the slates, a cloudburst filled the instrument with water and he belatedly realized that there was an organ behind the front pipes. The size of the repair bill was such that the contractor went out of business, leaving squabbling insurance companies in his wake.

The material from which front pipes are made is not always obvious. Zinc, 'spotted metal', polished 'tin metal' or 'flamed' copper? One church, seeking proposals for a new organ from four organbuilders, found that each one recommended a different material for the front pipes. Perhaps, if they had sought a fifth quotation, they might also have had a bid for 'plain metal' pipes covered in gold leaf, or even half-round dummy pipes made of wood, also gilded. And then there is the 1856 Gray & Davison organ in Leeds Town Hall, where the 32 ft front pipes are made of wrought iron!

The Romans used bronze, but since medieval times metal organ pipes have generally been made of alloys of tin and lead. The metal can be cast in sheets, ready for making up into pipes, and can be readily worked with hand tools and manipulated by a craftsman (known as the voicer) who takes the completed pipe and adjusts it to speak the correct note and tone colour. The tonal implications of pipe materials are outside the scope of this book but, where large front pipes are concerned, the main criteria are appearance, stability and cost. The more tin there is in the alloy, up to a maximum of 80 per cent, the stiffer the metal and the more attractive and long-lasting its appearance. The addition of a small impurity of copper yields a disproportionate increase in strength. Tin being many times the price of lead, there are economic incentives for minimizing its use. In practice, organbuilders in Spain, Holland and Germany have lavished more money on organ cases than British builders, combining polished 'tin metal' display pipes with the generous use of gold leaf on the woodwork. In Britain, late seventeenth- and eighteenth-century general practice was to use only about 20 per cent tin (so-called plain metal) and then to cover the front pipes in gold leaf, leaving the woodwork ungilded.

From 1870 to about 1960, there was almost no doubt which material to use. The majority of front pipes were made of zinc. Zinc is strong, relatively light, not expensive, not apt to collapse under its own weight and, if the upper and lower lips are let in with plain metal (80 per cent lead), the pipe can be made to speak a perfectly satisfactory note. The trouble is that bare zinc can look so shabby. How many organs are condemned out of hand because of the dull, flat, grey appearance of naked rows of zinc pipes?

The answer, of course, is to paint them. The idea of painted decoration on front pipes is a very old one; the seventeenth-century decoration on the plain metal pipes at Framlingham in Suffolk and at Gloucester

Painted decoration on front pipes showing an unusual treatment.
Manchester College Chapel, Oxford: decoration by William Morris, 1893.

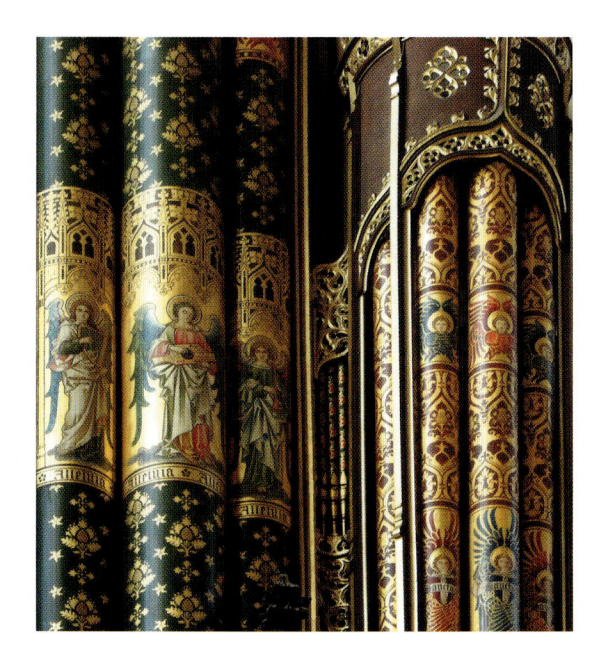

The 'rolls of linoleum' in Eton College Chapel. J. L. Pearson, 1882.

Embossed pipe. St Mary, Rickmansworth: Bryony Aldred, 2001. (Photo: Saxon Aldred)

'Barley-twist' embossed tin-metal pipe. (Photo: Shires Organ Pipes)

Cathedral still survives. This idea was revived in the nineteenth century, notably at Birmingham Town Hall, Durham Cathedral and Eton College Chapel, where J. L. Pearson's monumental zinc 32 ft front pipes have been jokingly described by generations of schoolboys as 'rolls of linoleum'.

After 1900 it became more common just to paint zinc pipes a single colour, generally a metallic gold. Such painting mimics the gilded plain metal front pipes usual in the eighteenth century but suffers from the fact that, if it is to remain smart, the paint needs to be renewed every 30 years or so. The metallic paint has to be sprayed on; it cannot be put on by hand without the brush-marks showing.

Gold leaf can be put on zinc pipes as well as those of tin–lead alloy but the zinc tends to corrode under the surface and the gilding does not last as long. Actually, the quality of surface finish of the zinc available to organbuilders today is very much better than in the past so one can now polish zinc and then lacquer it to delay oxidization. The 1993 Richard Bower organ in St Paul's Church, Harringay, London (see page 97) has this finish.

One can also decorate front pipes by embossing the metal itself. The sixteenth-century Gothic case from Scheemda, now in the Rijksmuseum in Amsterdam (see page 15), has many such pipes, as have a number of seventeenth-century organs in Britain by the Dallam and Harris families. The 1968 Mander organ in the chapel of Corpus Christi College,

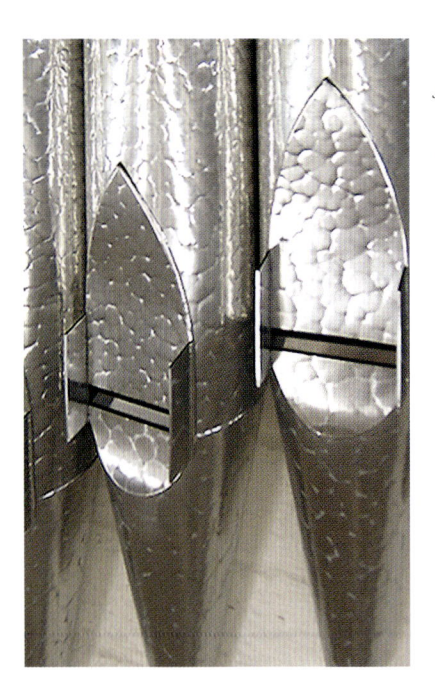

Spotted metal front pipes, 50 per cent tin.
(Photo: Shires Organ Pipes)

Gilded lips on polished tin-metal front pipes. Oakham Parish Church: Kenneth Tickell, 1995.

Cambridge, has some embossed pipes, as have a significant number of newer instruments. Polished tin-metal pipes (70–80 per cent tin) can be made to give jewel-like reflections by faceting the metal. A similar effect has been tried with zinc but the material is more difficult to work and the result is spoiled by the relatively matt surface.

Spotted metal front pipes (about 50 per cent tin, 50 per cent lead) are peculiar to Britain. The spots give the surface a distinctive glitter and they tone in well with Gothic-style woodwork. Although 8 ft spotted metal pipes cost slightly more than zinc ones, the finish is natural and doesn't have to be applied. The extra tin in spotted metal makes the pipes stronger than plain metal but not as strong as zinc or tin metal. The Hill firm occasionally made front pipes which appear to be spotted metal but are really zinc with spotted metal wrapped around the outside. The huge 32 ft front pipes in Sydney Town Hall, Australia, were made this way.

You can also wrap thin sheets of tin metal around zinc – the dummy west front pipes of the Quire organ at Southwell Minster had this applied in 1971. Tin-metal pipes used to be rare on organs in this country. Father Willis used tin metal for the 32 ft front pipes at the Royal Albert Hall in London, presumably for strength, and the curious 1695 Renatus Harris organ case in All Hallows, Twickenham, has original seventeenth-century tin pipes. The modern use of tin metal really dates from the neo-Baroque fashion of the 1960s, being copied from instruments made on the Continent, where the English preference for gilded front pipes never really held sway. Tin metal certainly looks much better on classical-style cases than spotted metal; there is the additional practical advantage that, because of the lower lead content, it takes much longer to go dull. If one wants a sumptuous effect, gilding the upper and lower lips of the mouths can be very effective. The back front of the 1995 Kenneth Tickell organ at Oakham

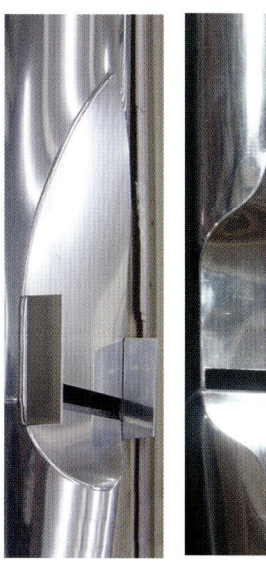

Bay-leaf   *Ogee*   *French mouth*

Pipe-mouth shapes
(Photos: Shires Organ Pipes)

Built-out pipe-mouths on 32 ft pipes. Sydney Town Hall, Australia: A. G. Hill, 1889.

Bars placed across pipe-mouths to aid prompt speech. Glyndebourne Organ Room, 1924.

Parish Church has plain tin-metal pipes whereas the otherwise similar transept front has the mouths gilded. Going from one side to the other, the comparison is instructive.

The shapes of the mouths of the pipes can also be used for decorative effect. Although the lower lip is nearly always semicircular, there is considerable scope for variety in the shape of the top lip which has to join the cylindrical upper part of the pipe to a flat surface. The lip can be pointed, in a shape known as the 'bay-leaf', or round-topped, sometimes called a 'French mouth'. The use of a projecting boss above the point of a bay-leaf mouth is generally attributed to 'Father' Bernard Smith in the late seventeenth century.

Most organ cases use only one shape of pipe-mouth, but a mixture of mouth types can be seen in seventeenth-century organ cases by the Dallam/Harris family. They were not the only ones – the 1834 William Hill case in Birmingham Town Hall has pointed top lips to

Pipes on show   11

the pipes in the flats and round-topped French mouths to the big 32 ft pipes in the towers. Later in the nineteenth century, Dr Arthur Hill usually used French mouths for his front pipes, as can be seen on the cases in Chichester and Peterborough cathedrals. In the larger pipes the lip is made of a separate piece of metal and the outline can be emphasized by having the top of the upper lip and the bottom of the lower lip curving forward and built out from the body of the pipe. Organbuilders sometimes jokingly refer to these as 'cow mouths'.

Sadly, organbuilders do sometimes spoil the appearance of front pipes. Just before the end of the nineteenth century, it was discovered that bass pipes could be made narrower yet still speak promptly if a bar (sometimes called a 'beard') was placed across the mouth. This is a useful aid for inside pipes but disastrous for the appearance of front pipes.

As noted in the last chapter, the scale of an organ case is determined by the longest pipe within it. The nominal length of this pipe (the distance from the top of the pipe down as far as the mouth) will either be 8 ft (for an organ with the lowest note as C two octaves below middle C) or can be 16 ft or even 32 ft in larger organs with stops pitched one or two octaves below the unison. Physical constraints sometimes dictate that a few of the longest pipes are placed inside the organ case but this can lead to problems of musical balance (the inside pipes will be softer) and will almost always increase the depth of the instrument.

The scale of the organ case also affects its proportions. The ratio between length and diameter of an organ pipe varies between treble and bass, the pipes becoming relatively fatter as they ascend in pitch. Thus a 32 ft case will always have more slender proportions than one of 16 ft and this will be more slender than one of 8 ft. In mathematical terms, the width of the longest pipe of a 16 ft case in proportion to its length will be about 15 per cent greater than the corresponding pipe of a 32 ft case. An 8 ft pipe will have proportions a further 15 per cent wider, and so on. Failure to understand this rule creates problems. For example, Sir Ninian Comper's otherwise notable organ case at Lound, Suffolk (see photograph on page 79) uses large case proportions on a small case, thus ensuring that the case pipes had to be false dummies.

It is possible to make case pipes slightly too long, cutting away the back so that the effective part of the pipe is shorter than it looks. This can be a useful trick if used in moderation but, if over-indulged, can yield a very false-looking effect with many pipes appearing to be speaking almost the same note or with clearly unnatural and elongated proportions. Gilbert Scott's organ cases are frequent offenders in this respect.

Apart from chamber organs, where other considerations apply, an organbuilder will design an organ case so that as many of the front pipes fill a musical purpose as possible, with the minimum number of dummies. Case designers who are not organbuilders have no inhibitions about over-length and dummies. The problem with dummies is that it is all too easy to distort their proportions because the designer is freed from the normal restrictions imposed by the pipes having to speak. A notable example is the

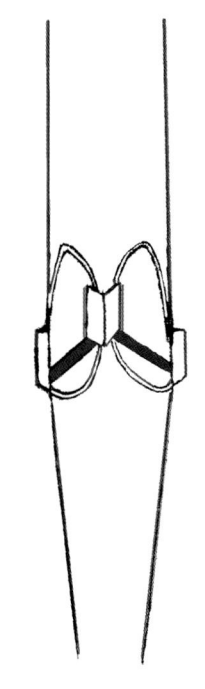

Corner pipe with two mouths. St Peter, Hindley, Lancashire: Austin and Paley, 1879.

12   The Box of Whistles

main case of Stephen Dykes-Bower's otherwise excellent design at Norwich Cathedral. He had a theory that no organ pipe should have a greater diameter than the half-round pilasters in the nave. As a result, the pipes in the main case are obvious dummies because they are too etiolated (too narrow compared with their length) to be capable of the right sound. A more amusing example of an unreal dummy occurs in the case designed by Austin and Paley for the famous Schulze organ at St Peter, Hindley, Lancashire. This has pipes in the side of the case as well as the front. The pipe adjacent to the post on the corner has two mouths at right angles, one facing each way. Perhaps it was just as well that it was not also required to speak.

3
GOTHIC AND RENAISSANCE ORIGINS

The development of the symmetrical organ case came at a time when Gothic architecture was already retreating in the face of the new ideas of the Renaissance, based on a revival of Greek and Roman forms. The result is that truly Gothic organ cases (as opposed to nineteenth-century Gothic Revival cases) are indeed rare. Constructed at the turn of the fourteenth and fifteenth centuries, the case of the Sion organ, with its crockets, pierced decoration and castellated towers, is entirely Gothic. A few later examples survive, all in Continental Europe.

One of the basic complications of organ case design is that all the pipes are of different lengths, as determined by the pitch of the note required. There are a number of devices to get round this problem. If we look again at the organ case at Sion, we can see two ways of coping with varying pipe-lengths. In the first place the case does not have a level top, the central portion being sloped more or less to follow the line of the pipe-tops. Second, the blank spaces at the tops of the towers are partially filled with delicate Gothic tracery.

In the early years of the next century, the case from Scheemda, Holland, now relatively accessible in the Rijksmuseum in Amsterdam, continued this tradition, with additional flamboyant decoration above the cornice to increase the vertical emphasis and the apparent height of the instrument. Notice, however, a development of this principle with the tracery following down the line of the pipe-tops and concealing their precise lengths with what we call a 'pipe-shade'. The variation in the height of the pipe-tops is also minimized by varying the length of the feet, with the longest pipes having the shortest feet, thus creating an attractive sloping mouth line and exaggerating the natural change in proportion between bass and treble pipes.

The last flowering of Gothic was the 'flamboyant' style, which never penetrated to England. A notable organ case influenced by this style, built towards the middle of the sixteenth century for the Nieuwe Zijdskapel in Amsterdam, is now in the Roman Catholic church in Jutphaas, near Utrecht. The pipe-shade tracery and the variable feet lengths found in the case at Scheemda are present here also, but the form of the organ case is developed further from the flat front of the organ at Scheemda, its

Two ways of coping with varying pipe-lengths: a sloping cornice and carved tracery 'pipe-shades'. Notre Dame de Valère, Sion, Switzerland, c.1400.
(Drawing by Herbert Norman)

Scheemda, Groningen, Netherlands: attributed to Johan Molner, Emden, 1526. Now in the Rijksmuseum.
(Photo: © Rijksmuseum Amsterdam)

Gothic and Renaissance origins 15

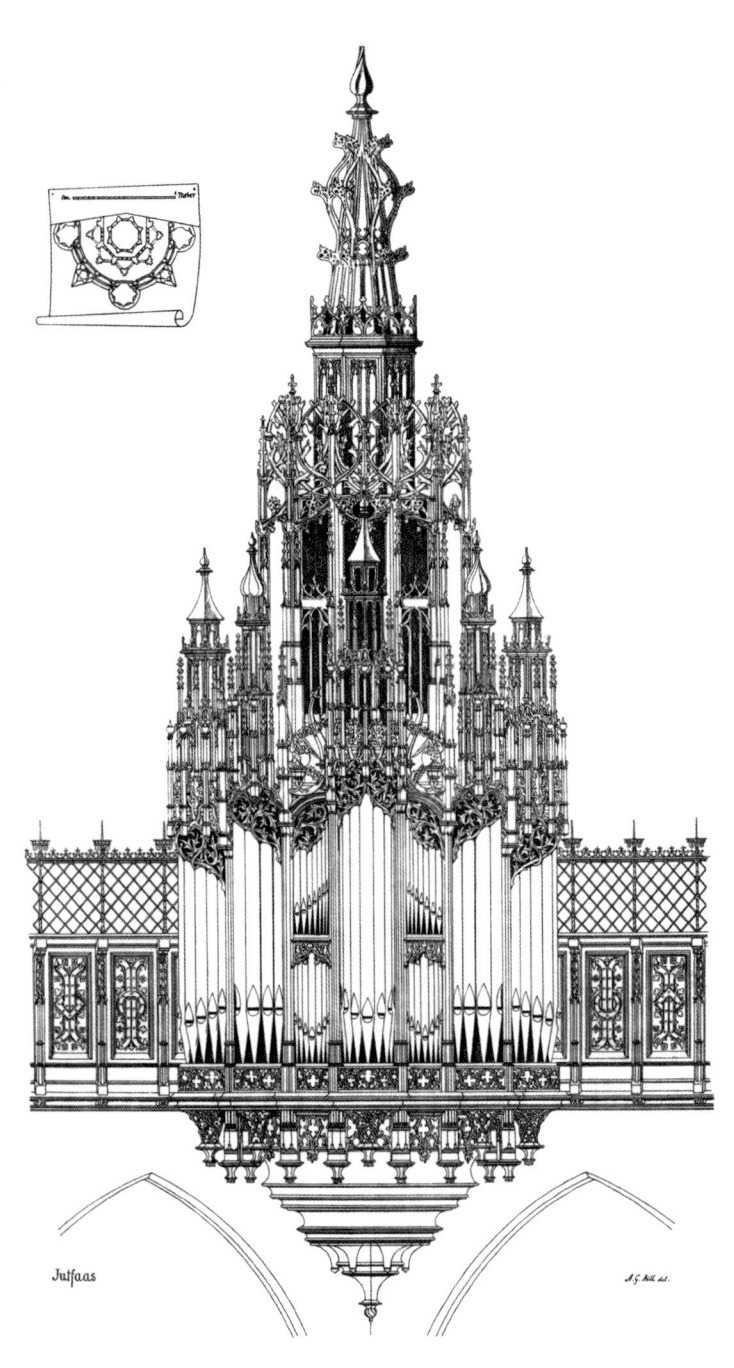

Nieuwe Zijdskapel, Amsterdam: attributed to Jan van Covelen, early to middle sixteenth-century. Now in Sint Nicolaas, Jutphaas, Netherlands. (Drawing by A. G. Hill)

semicircular plan losing any direct relationship to the layout of the interior. The projecting towers, alternately semicircular and V-shape, were an important precursor of what was to come. The original case doors are now missing.

One can draw fairly direct parallels from the Jutphaas and Scheemda cases to the oldest surviving organ case in Britain, which, despite its slightly uncertain provenance, is generally dated to about 1530. This can be found in St Stephen's Church at Old Radnor, close to the border between Herefordshire and Powys in Wales. Many Tudor organs were placed on rood lofts and so would have been destroyed by the iconoclasts who pulled the lofts down in the 1540s. The Old Radnor organ stands on the church floor and presumably this and the isolated location preserved it. It is the only remaining pre-1600 British organ case. The ideas of Renaissance architecture were slightly earlier in coming to Britain than to the Netherlands and although basically Gothic in form, some of the detail at Old Radnor shows early Mannerist influences. Indeed the lunette decoration of the cornice along the top of the instrument has strong parallels with some of the 1530s chimney decoration at the Château de Chambord in the Loire valley, France.

The Old Radnor case has many characteristics which have continued to be important in organ case design. First, one notices that, like

16   The Box of Whistles

The oldest surviving organ case in Britain: St Stephen, Old Radnor, Powys, c.1530. (Drawing by Herbert Norman)

the Sion organ, the case is 'waisted-in' at the bottom. As noted in Chapter 1, this follows the use of mechanism that allows the pipes to be spread over a greater distance than the width of the keyboard. Second, although the case is basically flat-fronted, following the shape of the soundboard and interior pipes behind it, the front pipes do not all stand in a single line. The longest stand in a 'V' formation, alternating with panels of smaller pipes. In this respect the Old Radnor case is an advance on the Sion and Scheemda cases, without going to the flamboyant extreme of Jutphaas. This alternation of 'towers' with 'flats' is the foundation of the architectural form and decoration of the organ case in most cultures.

We have already said that one of the basic complications of organ case design is that all the pipes are of different lengths. Another way of handling this problem is to provide an upper storey of small pipes in the flats to make the top of the case up to a level line. In this respect Old Radnor follows on from the example of the Scheemda organ. This was partly a reflection of the inside construction because, in Holland and Germany, organs acquired additional soundboards and pipes at a level above the main organ. The present interior of the Old Radnor organ is not original but it seems probable that, as in many later British instruments, there was no upper soundboard and the upper pipes did not speak.

The gradual infiltration of Renaissance detail into Gothic structures, as exemplified at Old Radnor, was also characteristic of European architecture in general. Only in Italy, where the Renaissance started, did it flower relatively completely, quickly eliminating Gothic influence. In fact because the Renaissance started earlier in Italy, it took over almost before large organ cases started to be built. Only one Gothic organ case, in San Petronio, Bologna, has survived. Dating from 1470, it was modified in the seventeenth century with a Baroque surround.

The classic Italian Renaissance organ case is very simple. It takes the basic flat-fronted construction, without projecting towers, seen at Sion, together with a level pipe-mouth line, and places it within an elaborate architectural frame with a bold cornice, sometimes surmounted by a strong pediment. Although tiny, the instrument

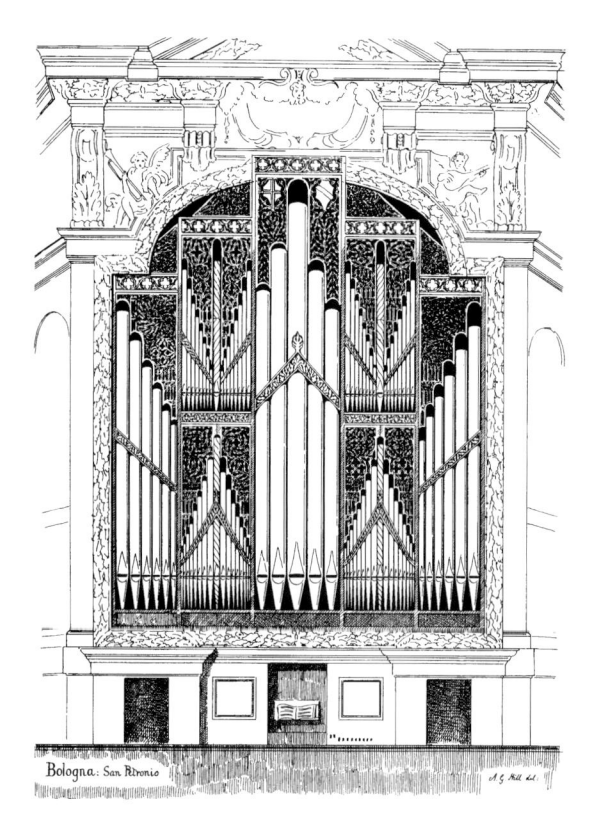

Reputed to be the only Gothic case in Italy: San Petronio, Bologna, Italy, c.1470. (Drawing by A. G. Hill)

in the chapel of the Palazzo Pubblico in Siena, dating from about 1500, is typical of a style which was to survive for several centuries.

The five-compartment front is a common Italian form, with bass pipes in three compartments and smaller pipes in two. Later instruments often had elaborate pipe-stays, decorated with swags. Another characteristic of Italian cases is the absence of pipe-shades, the natural asymmetric lengths of the pipes being left exposed, often beneath semicircular arches. With bass pipes distributed over three compartments and no variation in the length of the feet, there is often a marked difference in the lengths of adjacent pipes. Even though this style persisted so long with little change, except

Typical Italian Renaissance case: Chapel of the Palazzo Pubblico, Siena, Italy, c.1500. (Drawing by A. G. Hill)

in architectural detail, it had surprisingly little influence outside Italy and Spain until the second half of the twentieth century.

In England the Protestant bias against organs abated after the accession of James I in 1603. Thomas Dallam was a Catholic who had travelled to Istanbul to erect a clock-organ presented to Sultan Mehmed III by Queen

18   The Box of Whistles

Hatfield House, Hertfordshire: supplied from Holland by John Haan in 1608, decorated in England by Roland Bucket, and erected by Thomas Dallam. (Photo: © The Marquess of Salisbury)

paid for setting up the organ and Roland Bucket for the painted panels. Whoever made it, the case is certainly interesting. It combines Renaissance columns, a wealth of Jacobean strapwork and pipe-shades which, with their winged grotesque creatures, have both a Renaissance and a Gothic feeling.

More organs were built after the revival of High Church worship under Archbishop Laud (1633–45). The most important organ case from this period is the splendid case now known as the 'Milton' organ in Tewkesbury Abbey. Installed in Magdalen College, Oxford, in the 1630s by Robert Dallam (son of Thomas Dallam) but possibly made earlier, it owes its survival through the Commonwealth to the fact that it was requisitioned by Cromwell and moved to the Great Hall of Hampton Court, allegedly for his retinue to dance to. Although completely Jacobean in decoration, the case is fundamentally still of the same structural form as the largely Gothic case at Old Radnor, showing no influence whatever from the Renaissance cases which, by then, had been standard in Italy for over a century. Indeed, it could be argued that with its five towers, three semicircular and two V-shaped, there are definite echoes of the flamboyant Dutch Gothic case at Jutphaas. The drawing by Dr A. G. Hill dates from about 1890 and shows the case much as it is today, with the sides deepened to house a much larger organ.

Elizabeth and paid for by the Levant Company. In 1605–6 he built an organ for the chapel of King's College, Cambridge, although the case of that instrument seems not to have survived.

The case of the large chamber organ in Hatfield House, which has survived, is of less certain attribution. Surviving papers record payments to 'John Haan, a Dutchman' for its supply in 1608, although he appears to have been an agent, not a maker. Thomas Dallam was

Gothic and Renaissance origins | 19

Magdalen College, Oxford: Robert Dallam, c.1631. Now in Tewkesbury Abbey. (Drawing by A. G. Hill)

The clue to the original depth of the case can be seen in the relatively shallow returns of the central tower. The lower arcading of this case is peculiar to Tewkesbury, although it is less structurally perilous than it appears, as Hill omitted two of the supporting posts from his drawing. Uniquely among pre-Commonwealth instruments, the organ retains some original pipes including all the tin-metal front pipes, gilded and embossed and with varied mouth shapes.

The Magdalen College/Tewkesbury organ was originally a two-manual instrument with the Chair organ housed in a separate and smaller case in front of the main case. This is now thought to have survived in the form of the case of the one-manual organ now at St Nicholas, Stanford-on-Avon, Northamptonshire. The dummy chair case now in front of this instrument (which is just a screen to conceal the player) was added when the instrument arrived at Stanford-on-Avon in the eighteenth century. As is appropriate, it is simpler than the main case at Tewkesbury, having three towers. Nevertheless it still has a variety of shapes, with semicircular side towers and an unusual three-sided centre tower. Although the interior is derelict this case retains its original embossed front pipes with characteristically varied mouth shapes. The pipe-shades, shown here in Dr Hill's detailed drawings, are most dramatic and include mythical beasts that hark back to the Middle Ages.

There is something of a mystery over the west face of the organ case in King's College Chapel, Cambridge, as there is no documentary evidence of its arrival. It was formerly claimed to date from Thomas Dallam's organ of 1605 but it is now known that this stood on the floor and had a different case, more like the Magdalen College/Tewkesbury instrument.

The layout of the present case is unusual, with two strong towers at the corners and a vestigial tower between six flat compartments. The original angels on the towers were replaced

Former chair case from Magdalen College, Oxford: Robert Dallam, c.1631. Now the main case in St Nicholas, Stanford-on-Avon, Northamptonshire (dummy chair case a later addition). (Drawing by A. G. Hill)

by Gothic spires in the eighteenth century and by the present oversized figures in the nineteenth. It has been suggested that with the organ on a screen, the centre was kept low to maximize the view of the fan-vaulted ceiling. The perspective effect was achieved at the expense of some false length on the front pipes, possibly the first use of this potentially treacherous device. Similar receding perspective ideas occur in early seventeenth-century cabinets. Other Dallam family instruments with receding perspective include organs built in Quimper Cathedral, Brittany, in the 1640s, and in St George's Chapel, Windsor, constructed in 1661 after the restoration of the monarchy (see next chapter). As we will see in the next chapter, another organbuilder was at work at King's in 1661, so the King's west-face case seems likely to predate the Commonwealth. It could have originally been an east case supplied when the organ was moved to the screen, perhaps in the 1630s, and moved to face the other way later in the century when the present east case was made.

King's College Chapel, Cambridge (west face): attributed to Robert Dallam, before 1640. The impressive but out-of-scale angels are replacements by Gilbert Scott.

Gloucester Cathedral: chair case by Robert Dallam, 1641. (Adapted from a drawing by A. G. Hill)

Robert Dallam's final work before the Civil War was most probably the organ that he built for Gloucester Cathedral in 1641. Although the organ and its pipes were destroyed, the casework survives as the chair case of the present organ. Its complex form is quite breathtakingly original, with V-shaped side towers, gently curving flats and a most complex centre tower, with a single central pipe on a round base set within a much lower flat and rectangular structure. As with all Dallam's surviving work, the oak case is most beautifully made and the carving, also in oak, is of the very highest quality.

Catholic Dallam fled to Brittany in 1642, so ending a chapter in the development of the 'box of whistles'. In 1644, the government proclaimed an ordinance 'for the speedy demolishing of all organs, images and all matters of superstitious monuments . . . to remove offences and things illegal in the worship of God'. Soldiers vandalized organs; at Exeter 'they brake down the organs, and taking two or three hundred pipes with them in a most scorneful and contemptuous manner, went up and downe the streets piping with them'.

4
FATHER SMITH AND RENATUS HARRIS

The restoration of the monarchy in 1660 allowed everything to restart. There was a rush to restore dismantled organs where the parts had escaped destruction and to construct new ones where they had not. Organbuilders returned from abroad, inevitably with some fresh ideas, and the next hundred years or so were to constitute a golden age in organ case design and construction, one from which designers still draw inspiration, even today.

Although some family members remained in France, Robert Dallam returned quickly to make a new organ for St George's Chapel, Windsor. Although the case of this organ has not survived, a contemporary print shows its west face with a receding perspective strikingly similar to that of the surviving west face of the case at King's College, Cambridge.

Robert Dallam died in 1665. His daughter Katherine had married his protégé Thomas Harrison, who later changed his name to Thomas Harris, reputedly because his original name was the same as one of the signatories to Charles I's death warrant! Thus it was as Thomas Harris that he built the organ in Gloucester Cathedral in 1666. This still exists today, incorporating Dallam's 1641 case for the Choir organ. Harris's case is interesting, harking back to Tewkesbury with its overhanging side arches, yet forward-looking in its use of Roman arches and architectural broken pediments over the flat compartments, a device that he was to use again

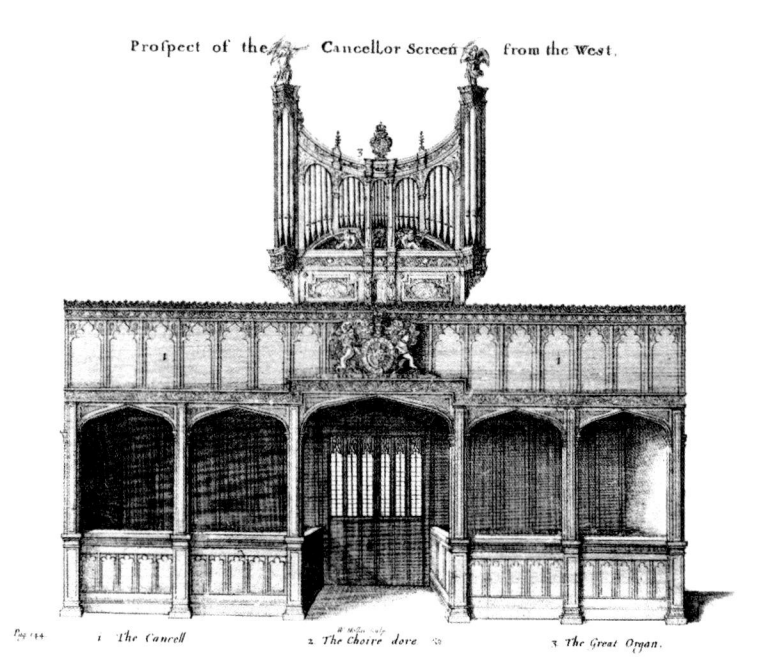

St George's Chapel, Windsor:
Robert Dallam, 1661.
(Engraving by Elias Ashmole, 1672)

West face *East face*

Gloucester Cathedral: main case by Thomas Harris, 1666, chair case by Robert Dallam, 1641.

and which foreshadowed the work of his son Renatus two decades or more later. The case has two faces, the present west-facing case having a curved pediment but being otherwise plainer, as it originally faced back into an aisle before the organ was moved to the screen in 1718. Close inspection will reveal that the pipe-shades on this side are not carved but of solid wood with painted decoration. Perhaps as a result of the post-Commonwealth rush, the Harris case is less well constructed than the little Dallam case, being mostly pine, painted and grained to look like oak. The Gloucester case retains its seventeenth-century front pipes, with their original painted decoration, as well as well over 200 interior pipes of the same date. Nevertheless the organ has been enlarged over the years, the case having been deepened and pipes added to the side in 1888 when, sadly, the side arches were also filled in. Much of the Pedal organ is hidden within the screen. The small grille in the lower part of the west case is modern, replacing nineteenth-century panelling.

Thomas Harris used a development of the Gloucester design for his next surviving major instrument, at St Sepulchre-without-Newgate, City of London. Here each flat is surmounted by one half of a broken pediment (curved, like the west face of Gloucester), either side of a central V-shaped tower. This case was, unfortunately, much altered in the twentieth century, the two side towers being reduced in height and the whole deprived of its lower casework below the impost. Additional gilding has been applied to the fine carving with a spectacularly heavy hand.

St Sepulchre-without-Newgate, City of London: Thomas Harris, 1676, chair case by Renatus Harris, 1702. Rearranged without lower casework in 1932. (Drawing adapted from John Norbury, 1877)

Chichester Cathedral: Thomas Harris, c.1677, chair case by John Byfield, 1725. Largely destroyed when the steeple collapsed in 1861. (Artist unknown)

Thomas Harris built at least two more cases to this design. The one at Chichester Cathedral was apparently destroyed when the cathedral tower collapsed in 1861. The Harris case at Newcastle Cathedral still retains its bold figure-work on top of the cornices and central tower but was drastically altered in 1891, when R. J. Johnson designed a 'matching' enlargement, replicating the outer towers, scaled up to take 16 ft pipes, placed either side and separated from the original case by narrow three-pipe flats. A chair case, added at the same time, was neatly done but the additional towers severely disturb the original proportions of the case.

The Dallam/Harris family did not have things all their own way, of course. One rival was Thomas Thamer of Cambridge. He appears to have been relatively old-fashioned where case design was concerned. There is a striking similarity between Dallam's 1631 Magdalen College/Stanford-on-Avon case (see page 21) and the three-tower case now in St Michael's Church, Framlingham, Suffolk. Built by Thamer for the chapel of Pembroke College, Cambridge in 1674, it moved to Framlingham in 1707 and some of Thamer's pipes remain in the present instrument. With its three-sided central tower supported by scroll brackets and false

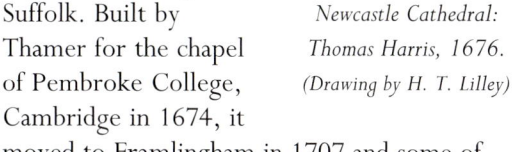

Newcastle Cathedral: Thomas Harris, 1676. (Drawing by H. T. Lilley)

Father Smith and Renatus Harris   25

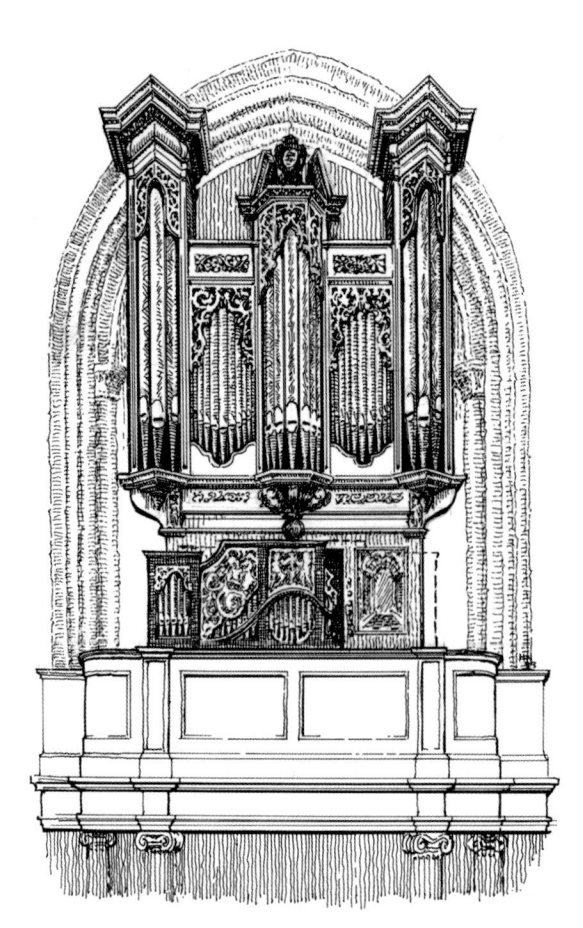

Pembroke College, Cambridge: Thomas Thamer, 1674. Installed in St Michael, Framlingham, Suffolk, in 1707 (dummy chair case not original). (Drawing by Herbert Norman)

False perspective lower panel. (Photo: Jim Berrow)

perspective lower panels, the design harks back to the 1630s. Again there is a vestige of Gothic feeling about the pipe-shades and the painted decoration on the front pipes. As at Stanford-on-Avon, the dummy chair case which acts as a screen behind the player was probably added when the organ came to its present destination.

In 1665, the same year that Harris built the Gloucester organ, John Loosemore built the very distinctive instrument in Exeter Cathedral. Not too much is known about Loosemore save that he combined being organbuilder with his position as Clerk of the Works to the cathedral. Standing boldly in its original position on the pulpitum, the case has east and west faces with a chair case on the east face; the similar chair case now on the west face is a late nineteenth-century

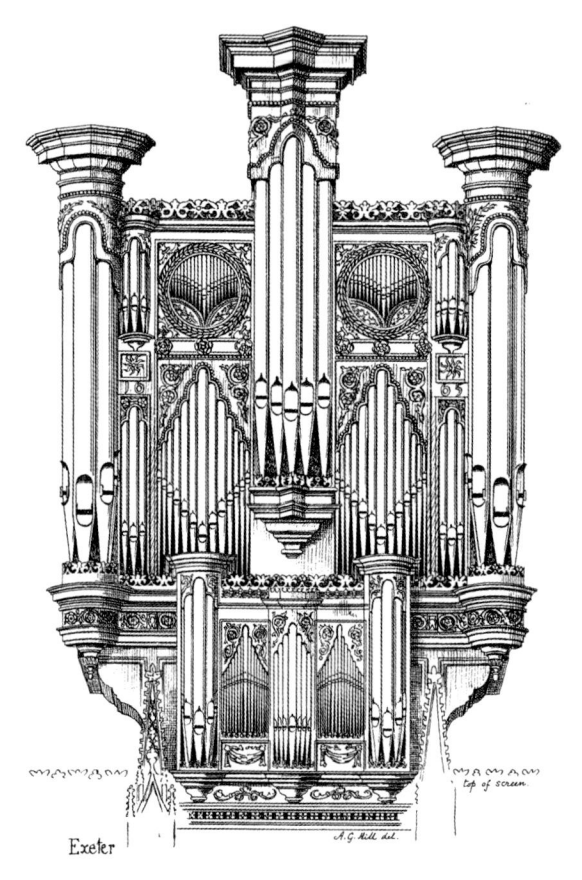

Exeter Cathedral, east face, at original height: John Loosemore, 1665. (Drawing by A. G. Hill)

26   The Box of Whistles

replica. The east face in particular is a riot of invention. The centre tower is rectangular with a V-shaped projection for the central pipe but the outer towers go beyond a semicircle and have circular caps. The upper storeys of the flats have a completely different shape from the lower, being set in circular panels surrounded by wreaths. The relatively narrow outer towers are bolstered by two-storey subsidiary compartments, with the upper ones forming curved corner towers. There is also an unbelievable variety of foot-lengths, with the main towers following the usual rule of having the longest pipe with the shortest foot, the middle tower of the chair case and the upper flats of the main case all having feet of the same length (but with a curved and sloping tip-board to the round compartments). The flats of the chair case are particularly startling, with the difference in pipe lengths being exaggerated by a rising mouth line. The original front pipes were of embossed tin but these, sadly, were replaced in the nineteenth century.

The identity of the designer of the east face of the organ in King's College, Cambridge, is something of a mystery, partly because the College Fellows seem to have kept chopping and changing organbuilders. The chair case was made in 1661 by Lancelot Pease before he emigrated to Dublin, where his organ case in the Examination Hall of Trinity College still exists. Thomas Thamer worked on the organ in 1678 and Renatus Harris (son of Thomas Harris) in 1688. In the 1660s the organist was Henry Loosemore, brother of the John Loosemore who built the Exeter organ, so the round towers at the corners of the case (as at Exeter) may be no coincidence. It has also been suggested that the goat-legged satyrs and the carved reliefs of King David in the lower part of the case are pre-Commonwealth in design, possibly dating from the same period as the west face, perhaps damaged by Cromwell's troops and later reused.

King's College Chapel, Cambridge (east face): chair case by Lancelot Pease, 1661, main case possibly by Renatus Harris, 1688. (Drawing by A. G. Hill)

Father Smith and Renatus Harris

On the other hand, the even band of carving above the flats is reminiscent of that on the Harris organ case made for Jesus College, Cambridge, in 1689 and now at Little Bardfield, Essex, so Harris may have been its author, especially as the tiny central tower and sloping tip-board of the flats are similar to an instrument built by his grandfather, Robert Dallam, for Plestin, Brittany. Whatever its provenance, the boldness of the design of the King's College case and the quality of its carving make it an exemplar. The presence of the royal coat of arms on the central tower and the crowns on the outer towers of both main and chair cases was, of course, a political statement appropriate to the Restoration. It became quite a common custom, lasting about a century, to have a crown over the centre tower of an organ case and an archbishop's mitre over each of the two side towers, as, for example, in the 1715 case at Birmingham Cathedral.

The King's College organ has grown over the years to become a very substantial instrument and the case has been correspondingly deepened, with the east front hard up against the back of the chair case and the player moved to the north side. The original embossed front pipes were replaced in the nineteenth century.

A typical Smith three-tower case, in St Nicholas, Deptford, London: Bernard Smith, 1697. Destroyed in 1941. (Drawing by H. T. Lilley)

The crown and archbishop's mitre in St Philip's Cathedral, Birmingham: Thomas Swarbrick, 1715.

The Dallam/Harris family encountered another notable rival in 1667 when Bernard Smith came to London. Trained in Germany, he moved first to Holland (where he built an organ for the Grote Kerk in Edam which still exists) and then to London, perhaps hoping to capitalize on the destruction wrought by the Great Fire the previous year. He later became generally known as 'Father Smith' to distinguish him from his nephews Christian and Gerard Smith who, separately, set up in competition. Smith established a reputation quite quickly, building an instrument for St Margaret's, Westminster, in 1675.

The following year Smith built an organ for the University Church of St Mary the Virgin in Oxford with a three-tower case which has remained the popular image of a Smith case, copied many times right up to the present day, including the

St Katharine Cree, City of London: Bernard Smith, 1686.
(Drawing by A. G. Hill)

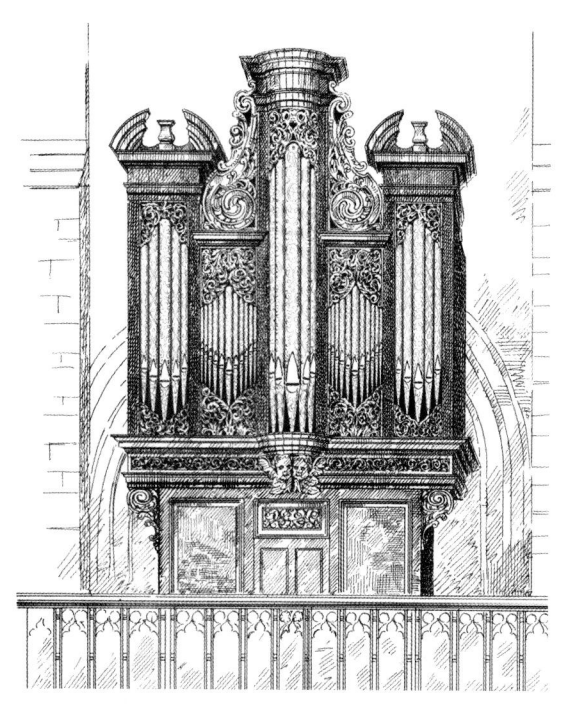

Windsor Castle private chapel: Bernard Smith, c.1702. Now in Finedon Parish Church, Northamptonshire.
(Drawing by A. G. Hill)

present Oxford case which is a modern pastiche replacement. The design is based on three semicircular towers, the largest in the centre, with double-storey flats between the towers.

The 1686 instrument at St Katharine Cree in the City of London has single-storey flats and, with its curved pediments above the flat compartments, is one of the most 'architectural' of Smith's cases. Common to all, however, are the carved cherubs' heads supporting the towers, fine carving along the impost and carved brackets supporting the overhang at the sides. The St Katharine Cree case shows signs of last-minute design changes while under construction, with towers not quite lining up with the impost. The organ was formally approved by Henry Purcell.

The final fling of the three-tower Smith case style was also in a more architectural vein but with the pediments placed over the towers instead of the flats, with flamboyant scroll-work in between. It is thought that the organ now in Finedon Parish Church, Northamptonshire, was made in about 1702 for the private chapel at Windsor Castle (there is a royal coat of arms on the central tower which has been dated between 1702 and 1707). It was moved to Finedon in 1717 by Bernard Smith's nephew, Gerard Smith.

The front of the main case at Durham Cathedral, which formerly stood on a screen, is now fixed to the wall of the south nave aisle of the cathedral. It is of the four-tower form which, at the time, was almost unique to Bernard Smith in Britain (though many-towered cases are common in France, the Albi Cathedral organ having nine towers). Another surviving Smith four-tower case is that built for Christ Church Cathedral, Oxford. The chair case is a Victorian addition and the proportions of the

University Church of Great St Mary, Cambridge: Bernard Smith, 1698.

Trinity College Chapel, Cambridge: Bernard Smith and Christopher Shrider, 1708.

main case were changed when it was lifted to allow the insertion of a Swell division below the impost by Joseph von Glatter-Götz (Rieger Orgelbau, 1979). The main case of the organ Smith built in 1699 for Inigo Jones's Whitehall Banqueting House (at the time when it was turned into a chapel) was moved in 1890 to the chapel of St Peter ad Vincula, within the Tower of London, losing its chair case in the process. It has recently had a new organ placed inside it, with replacement front pipes. Smith also made a four-tower case, probably in 1700, for Eton College Chapel. This now stands in Hawkesyard Priory, near Rugeley, little altered but somewhat neglected.

Cambridge boasts two four-tower cases by Smith. That at the west end of Great St Mary, the University Church, was built in 1698. It differs slightly from the others in the coupling of the two centre towers by a common cornice; the centre panel below this cornice originally contained a clock. It never had a chair case, the pipes of the Choir organ being accommodated in a deepened main case which was originally all in front of the tower arch, forward of its present position. The present plain-metal front pipes are copies of the original (which were probably gilded) whereas the carving would not originally have been gilded.

The other four-tower Smith case in Cambridge is in Trinity College Chapel. It is based on the three-tower case now at Finedon and was probably Smith's last, finished in 1708 after his death by Christopher Shrider, his

*Bristol Cathedral:
Renatus Harris, 1685.
(Drawings by H. T. Lilley)*

East front

West front

son-in-law. Like Finedon, the side towers are flat and non-projecting to allow the broken curved pediments above the pipe-caps. The organ stands on a screen and the main case is therefore double-sided. This case was widened to six towers by Sir Arthur Blomfield in 1870 and later additions above the top of the case concealed by curtains hung from the ceiling! It was restored to its original width in 1976 although the case is still deeper than as made. Both the backward continuation of the brackets of the side overhang and the new tin-metal front pipes with gilded mouths are in the current fashion but are not historical; the original pipes would have been gilded all over.

The Dallam/Harris family lost much work to Smith, but when Thomas Harris's son René (born in France during the Commonwealth) took charge of the business in 1683 (he latinized his name to Renatus) he set about reviving the family fortunes. Smith had contracted to build an organ for the Temple Church in London but Harris persuaded the Benchers to allow him also to build an organ for them and to let them choose which they wanted to keep. Both organs were finished in 1684 and there were concerts by distinguished musicians to help the Benchers choose. The 'Battle of the Organs' raged for three years but Smith's organ (which incorporated several significant musical novelties) eventually won. Its case, sadly, was destroyed in 1843. Renatus Harris had to take his organ away; parts were used in an organ for Christ Church Cathedral, Dublin, and what is reputed (possibly wrongly) to be its case is now in St John's Church, Wolverhampton. Harris was nevertheless established in his career and, though famously awkward in his business dealings, proved to be a very imaginative organbuilder who introduced many novel ideas into his cases.

Renatus Harris's first major commission was at Bristol Cathedral in 1685, where the east front of the double-sided case has three semicircular towers and the convex 'round-shouldered' cornices over the flats, based on his father's case at Chichester. The matching west front has a more complex design with fluted columns on either side of the flats and curved pediments set below the cornices above them. Both cases had the pipes in the flats set within semicircular arches, the same design as that used by his father 20 years before at Gloucester Cathedral. When the Bristol screen was taken down in 1860 the two fronts were placed side

The Queen's Chapel, Whitehall, London: Renatus Harris, 1686. The main case has been in St James, Piccadilly, London since 1691. (Photo: Andrew Freeman/British Organ Archive)

Chair case from the Queen's Chapel, Whitehall, London: attributed to Renatus Harris, 1686. Now in St Mary Woolnoth, City of London.

by side between the columns of the north aisle, losing the crown and archbishops' mitres which formerly stood on the towers and the figure-carving which Harris probably also provided above the cornices.

Harris developed his 'round-shouldered' case for the Queen's 'popish' Chapel in Whitehall in 1686. On the death of James II it was given to St James's Church, Piccadilly, London, where it was re-erected in 1691 and still remains. Harris developed the flat compartments as two storeys, with the upper one running up into the curved cornice. The case is notable for a riot of angels and trumpet-blowing *putti* above the towers and cornices, believed to be the work of Grinling Gibbons. Harris became known for his figure-work – reclining angels above the cornices – in contrast to Smith who tended to stick to fancy scroll-work. Harris cases also feature pierced carving along the impost as well as the usual cherub-heads supporting the towers. The chair case now at Piccadilly is a pastiche dating from 1852; it is the author's theory that the long-disused case at the west end of St Mary Woolnoth, City of London, is the original chair case from Whitehall. The massive louvred swell-box now projecting over the Piccadilly case was a late nineteenth-century addition. The case and organ have been neglected in recent years.

In 1690 Harris produced a development of this 'round-shouldered' design for Christ Church, Newgate Street, City of London, with the pipes in the lower storey of flats placed within an oval panel and surrounded by carving. This device, perhaps derived from Loosemore's case at Exeter, was to recur in Harris's work. Another example followed, at St Bride, Fleet Street, in 1694. Both cases were destroyed by bombing in World War Two. However, the similar case made two years later, in 1696, for

St Andrew Undershaft, City of London: Renatus Harris, 1696.

St Clement, Eastcheap, City of London: Renatus Harris, 1696. Rearranged without lower casework in 1936.

St Andrew Undershaft, also in the City of London, still exists, moved in the nineteenth century from the west end to the south side of the chancel and shorn of its ornaments on top of the central tower. There is another, also shorn of ornaments, in St Mary, Dublin (now a restaurant!).

In the same year as the Undershaft organ, Harris followed up with a really original and strange design. The case at St Clement, Eastcheap, City of London, has a short, flat, central tower above a very large oval flat compartment which stretches the whole width of the case between the two outer towers. The centre tower is flanked by two-storey flats, the upper storey conventional beneath a curved cornice reminiscent of Father Smith's three-tower design. The lower storey, however, contains two smaller oval panels. The whole effect is bizarre. The Eastcheap case remains in approximately its original position at the west end, but, now built into the door case beneath, it has lost the casework below the impost as well as the crown and mitres above the towers.

One artistic question posed by the organ cases of both Renatus Harris and Father Smith is that, before 1700, nearly all of them were installed in existing Gothic buildings. Yet, as children of their time, these cases incorporated the latest Renaissance-based furniture styles. Despite this apparent anachronism, artistic opinion, both then and now, accepts them as entirely

Father Smith and Renatus Harris   33

appropriate to the buildings in which they stand. The reason for this is surely that the organ case in Britain evolved from the original fifteenth-century Gothic framework, changing its decoration in response to contemporary architectural fashion, but retaining the same fundamental Gothic structure. Had we copied the Renaissance case as it evolved in Italy, many more artistic problems would have arisen.

The question of what was appropriate to a new building was to come to a head at St Paul's Cathedral, London. Father Smith was awarded the contract but, contrary to previous practice, did not design the organ case. Sir Christopher Wren designed everything in St Paul's and that included the organ case. He faced a difficult problem. Although in many ways a Gothic building structurally, the appearance of St Paul's is basically Italian Baroque. A flat Italian case set against one of the Choir arches would have been entirely in keeping and there is some evidence that he explored such a position for the instrument but found his arcade not lofty enough for it to be practicable. The liturgical needs of the English Church also called for a choir screen, so he put the organ on the screen (Loosemore's layout at Exeter, used later by Smith in the cathedrals at Oxford and Durham).

Instead of creating an elaborate confection of towers and flats, as would have been the practice in France or Germany at the time, Wren made a revolutionary choice. He decided to construct the organ case as an architectural feature, integrating it closely with the screen on which it sat. To this end it has the simplest possible outline, with two towers only and a single large flat between them with an almost rococo curved cornice. The towers do

St Paul's Cathedral, London: Sir Christopher Wren, 1697. Organ by Bernard Smith. Shown in its original position on the choir screen, but without the sliding screens originally fitted to keep construction industry dust out of the interior. (Drawing by Herbert Norman)

not project, the front being in a straight line, and there are no side overhangs. Like a number of architect's cases since, its design is quite 'woody', Wren using the spaces thus created for a luxurious display of the woodcarver's art, all carried out to the highest possible standard by Grinling Gibbons. Although Wren originally conceived the chair case with just an oval flat and no towers, he eventually settled on what is effectively a miniature of the main case.

Although the 'damned box of whistles' story is now thought to be a nineteenth-century invention, it is highly likely that there was friction between Wren and Smith. Unlike Renatus Harris, Smith had a reputation for straightforwardness but it must have been very irksome for him not to have everything under his own authority. One fundamental problem, which has cropped up many times since, is that architects always want to control the dimensions of the bass pipes which stand on show in the front of the case. Although the foot-length (the tapered part of the pipe between the tip and the mouth) can be varied fairly readily, all the other dimensions are determined by the tone and the pitch of the note which that pipe has to speak. Architects often have difficulty in realizing that these are fundamental and non-negotiable.

We do not see the St Paul's organ case today in the way Wren intended. In 1860 F. C. Penrose decided he wanted the screen out of the way so that the cathedral would look like one long parish church. The organ had to be moved. After several makeshift measures and false starts, in 1872 the case was divided in two and placed in its present position either side of the arch between dome space and Choir, with a second replica chair case provided so that both sides would match. Viewed sideways on (not ideal for the projection of sound down the cathedral), the depth of the case each side had to be kept to a minimum with the result that the case now accommodates less than half the organ, the remainder being hidden away within the north choir screen and in the quarter domes above. There were proposals in 1972 for the organ to return to Wren's original position but, so far, these have not borne fruit.

The St Paul's Cathedral organ case was almost a 'one-off'. The case at St Mildred, Bread Street, City of London, made nearly 40 years later in 1745 and destroyed in 1940, had the same silhouette and the early eighteenth-century case

St Paul's Cathedral, London:
afternoon sun on a riot of Grinling Gibbons carving.

made for the Foundling Hospital, London and now in St Andrew, Holborn, also has the same general form although very different decoration. Apart from these two, the St Paul's case had no general influence on organ case design save in one feature only: the absence of side overhang of the impost and upper casework above the lower casework. This point was picked up straight away by Renatus Harris whose cases after 1700 all had straight sides. Nevertheless, we shall see in the next chapter that case design in Britain remained remarkably conservative in the next century and that the work of both Father Smith and Renatus Harris remained an inspiration to their successors for far longer than could have been expected.

5
QUEEN ANNE AND GEORGIAN

Pembroke College Chapel, Cambridge: Charles Quarles, 1708. (Photo: Mander Organs)

St James, Garlickhythe, City of London: John Knopple, 1718.

Father Smith died early in the new century but instruments in his style were made by others even before his death. The organs in the chapels of Christ's College and Pembroke College, Cambridge were formerly ascribed to Smith but are now known to have been supplied by Charles Quarles in 1705 and 1708, with similar main cases of vaguely Smith style, although with V-shaped outer towers. The chair case at Pembroke College is unique in having two flats side by side without a tower in between.

Whether this was really intended or merely the result of a last-minute omission of a central tower is open to question.

The other Smith-like case was that installed by John Knopple at St James, Garlickhythe, City of London in 1718. This is a four-tower case so close to Smith's style that critics have speculated on its origins. Knopple had worked for Smith so

36   The Box of Whistles

*St Lawrence Whitchurch,
Little Stanmore, Middlesex:
Gerard Smith, 1717.
(Photo: Goetze & Gwynn / Matthew Crowthers)*

*Emmanuel College, Cambridge:
chair case attributed to Renatus
Harris, 1686. (Adapted from a
photograph by John Brennan)*

it seems likely that either he had made Smith's cases himself or that he knew the craftsmen who had made the originals. The important difference is the very heavy-looking pediment above the two central towers which does not relate well to the rest of the case. It has been suggested that this is in the style of Nicholas Hawksmoor and could have been added at his behest.

Smith's nephews were also working in a similar style. Christian Smith fell out with his uncle in 1690 and, working separately, made an organ for St Peter's Church, Tiverton, Devon, probably in 1696. Although moved, the case has been little altered and follows Bernard Smith's standard design with three semicircular towers and two-storey flats. The other nephew, Gerard Smith, built the organ in St Lawrence Whitchurch, Little Stanmore, Middlesex in 1717. This amazing church was rebuilt at the charge of James Bridges, Duke of Chandos (who hired Handel as his musician in residence), with interior decoration in the nearest thing we have to Italian Baroque. As the Duke's private pew occupied the west gallery, the organ stands at the east end in a stage-like apse with a Grinling Gibbons screen as proscenium arch. The case survives, complete with original front pipes. Despite its surroundings it was conservative in design, closely resembling the 1689 case from Jesus College, Cambridge (now at Little Bardfield, Essex) generally attributed to Renatus Harris and the 1686 chair case in Emmanuel

All Hallows, Lombard Street, City of London: Renatus Harris, 1701. Now in All Hallows, Twickenham, Middlesex.

Bath Abbey: Abraham Jordan, 1708. Destroyed in the nineteenth century. (Detail from a print 1750 by James Vertue)

College Chapel, Cambridge, often attributed to Smith but actually more in the Harris style. Gerard Smith's workmanship at Little Stanmore is not up to the Smith or Harris standard of finish; the two tower caps are of slightly different construction, presumably made by different people.

Renatus Harris was some 20 years younger than Bernard Smith and continued to develop his casework styles after 1700. The organ built for All Hallows, Lombard Street, City of London in 1701, with its short central tower above a large round flat compartment, is a clear development and simplification of his Eastcheap case of five years before. It seems to have been his first with straight sides, without overhang, following the example of Wren's case at St Paul's Cathedral.

The All Hallows case travelled, with many other fittings of the church, to a new 1930s building, All Hallows, Twickenham, Middlesex, and is relatively intact. It appears to have been the last case of the period to make use of bright tin-metal front pipes instead of a more lead-rich alloy, painted or gilded.

A new competitor appeared early in the eighteenth century in the shape of Abraham Jordan. The 1708 organ in Bath Abbey is traditionally ascribed to Jordan, although a near-contemporary print shows the case to be almost identical to the Harris case now at Twickenham. The similarity may be explained by the fact that, elsewhere, Jordan is known to have used an outside cabinetmaker for his casework. The Bath case did not survive the Scott restoration of the

*St Magnus the Martyr, Lower Thames Street,
City of London: Abraham Jordan, 1712.
(Adapted from a drawing by John Norbury, 1877)*

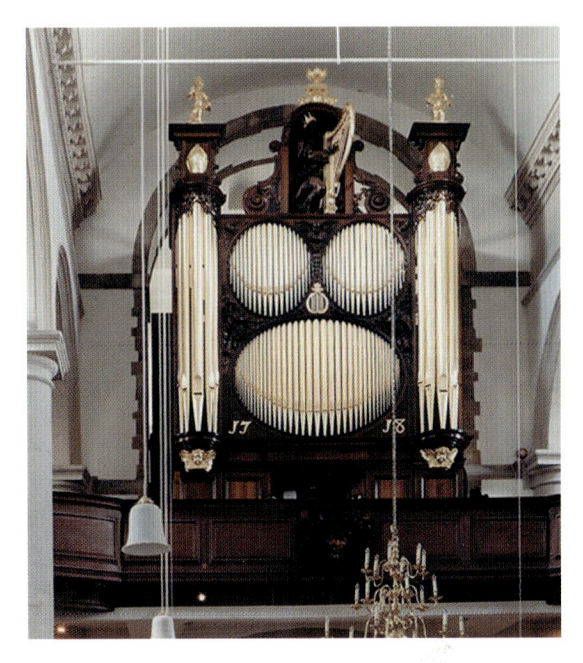

*St Thomas's Cathedral, Portsmouth (east face):
Abraham Jordan, 1718. (Photo: Nicholson & Co.)*

abbey in 1868 although the statue of King David from above the case towers remains in the building and is a fine example of early eighteenth-century carving.

Jordan really established his reputation with another new organ in the City of London, that at St Magnus the Martyr, Lower Thames Street. Built in 1712, this instrument incorporated important musical developments but also had a most unusual case for Britain. There is some suggestion that Jordan's family had Iberian connections (in the liquor trade) and had copied an Iberian mechanical invention (the swellbox, allowing the player to use a lever pedal to vary the volume of sound). At St Magnus, parts of the case, with its flat front and architectural form, seem in some respects to follow Iberian practice (which had, in places, been influenced by Italian ideas). The main case, of three rectangular and almost flat towers with single-storey flats, is crowned with a single large curved pediment, broken by a separate upper-storey case consisting of a single flat of obviously dummy pipes under a curved Baroque pediment. This was a 'one-off' and such a two-storey case did not reappear in the British organ for nearly another 80 years.

Jordan went back to raiding Renatus Harris's ideas for his 1718 organ for St Thomas's Parish Church, Portsmouth (now the cathedral). With its one large and two small oval panels, this curiously inelegant case is known locally as the 'Laughing Monkey'. Certainly, it is a clear development of the case at St Clement, Eastcheap. It even has a statue of King David

Queen Anne and Georgian 39

Grosvenor Chapel, Mayfair, London: Abraham Jordan II, 1732.

St Mary the Virgin, Oxford: Bernard Smith, 1676. (From a drawing by H. T. Lilley)

with a harp (like Bath). It might not have been mere plagiarism, of course. Both cases might have come from a common cabinetmaking source, as was to happen later in the century.

Abraham Jordan's son, also Abraham, was not above borrowing ideas from Father Smith as well. His 1732 case at the Grosvenor Chapel, Mayfair, London, is clearly based on Smith's three-tower/two-storey flat design first used at Oxford 56 years before, save that the central tower is flat, not semicircular, and the sides do not overhang.

To return to the beginning of the century, in 1702, the year after the All Hallows case, and just down the road at St Edmund, Lombard Street, Renatus Harris created a surprisingly simple design where the case consists of a very large flat with a convex top between two relatively small towers. A single curved pediment spans all three compartments. The

St Edmund, Lombard Street, City of London: Renatus Harris, 1702. Now perched above a doorway with the royal arms in front of the former console doors.

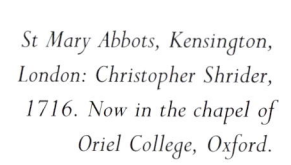

St Mary Abbots, Kensington, London: Christopher Shrider, 1716. Now in the chapel of Oriel College, Oxford.

40   The Box of Whistles

base-line of the pediment is broken except for the two ends, so that the two towers look as if they are columns supporting the pediment. This design also appears to have been a 'one-off', not repeated elsewhere. This case still exists, partnered by a twin, copied when the organ was enlarged in 1880. Christopher Shrider copied some elements of this design for his curious and unsatisfactory 1716 case for St Mary Abbots, Kensington (now in the chapel of Oriel College, Oxford, with minor changes). This has a similar large flat in the upper storey and round-topped compartments either side of a small concave compartment (like a niche) with dummy pipes all the same length.

Just after the two Lombard Street cases, Renatus Harris's extraordinary range of invention led to yet another

St Botolph, Aldgate, City of London: Renatus Harris, 1702–4.

Queen Anne and Georgian 41

design, one that was to be widely copied over more than 50 years. With perhaps a nod to the ornaments above the flats in his earlier case at Hereford Cathedral, now long gone, the main feature of his organ for St Botolph, Aldgate, City of London, was the 'gabled' cornice to the flats, the upper storeys of which neatly echo the shape of the lower storey. This organ also exhibits the extremely fine figure-carving which was a feature of Harris's work.

Harris developed the design further when, in 1710, he produced the first four-manual organ in Britain, for Salisbury Cathedral. The exuberant superstructures added height to match a tall building and the curved plan of the flat compartments of the chair case was a precursor of future developments. The Salisbury case does not survive; it was replaced by an organ with a 'Gothick' case in 1792. Neither does the similar case of the organ in St Dionis, Backchurch, City of London, built in collaboration with his son John Harris in 1724. This was moved in the nineteenth century and then destroyed in the wartime blitz.

Renatus Harris's competitors and successors also made 'gabled' cases. Thomas Swarbrick had been apprenticed to Harris but moved away

Salisbury Cathedral: Renatus Harris, 1710. Destroyed in 1792.

St Philip's Cathedral, Birmingham: Thomas Swarbrick, 1715. (From a contemporary watercolour)

from London and, in 1715, built a substantial organ for St Philip's Church, Birmingham (now the cathedral). Originally at the west end, the case is now rather less visible, jammed between two pillars on the north side of the Choir. It is particularly grand, with 'flats' which are V-shaped on plan (as seen from above), between semicircular towers and an especially bold set of crown and mitres on the tower caps. A much-altered Swarbrick case also survives at St Mary, Warwick.

Cases with gabled flats were also used by Jordan (including St Helen, Abingdon, Oxfordshire, 1725, which still exists) and by John Harris and his brother-in-law John Byfield. There is a surviving case dating from 1729 with

St Philip's Cathedral, Birmingham, present day appearance.

Chichester Cathedral: chair case by John Byfield, 1725. Largely destroyed when the steeple collapsed in 1861. (Artist unknown)

St Leonard, Shoreditch, London: Richard Bridge, 1754. (Drawing by Herbert Norman)

Queen Anne and Georgian 43

*South European rococo style,
St George's Abbey, Ochsenhausen, Germany:
Joseph Gabler, 1728–34. (Photo: Orgelbau Kuhn and Orgelbau Klais)*

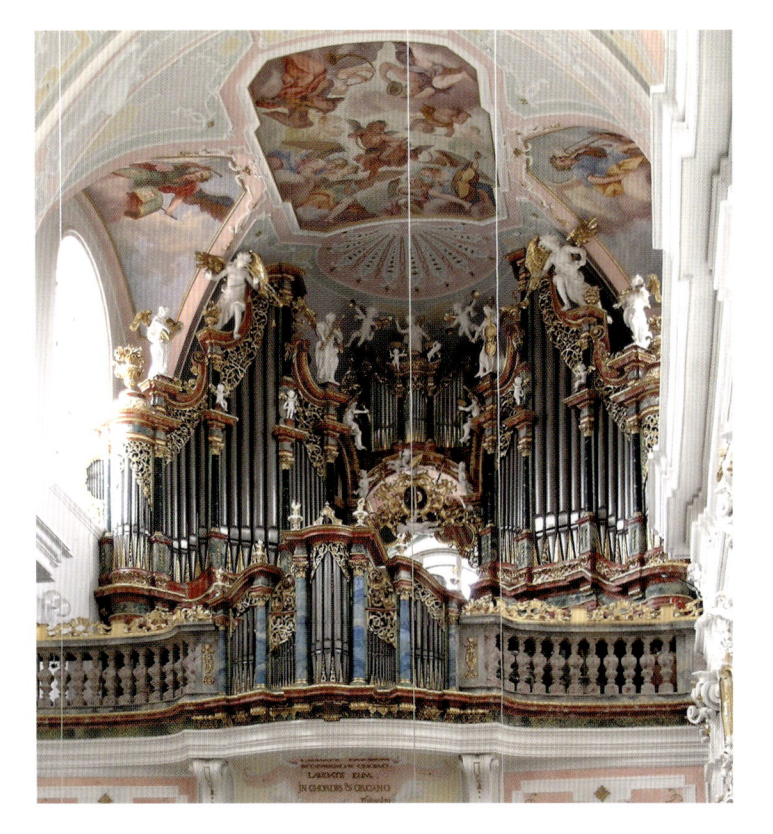

*Salisbury Cathedral: chair case,
Renatus Harris, 1710.
Destroyed in 1792.*

original front pipes, at St Mary, Shrewsbury, thought to be by Harris and Byfield. Finally, Richard Bridge (who had trained with Renatus Harris) used this design for the case in St Leonard, Shoreditch, London, in 1754. Complete with crown and mitres above the tower caps (nearly a century after the Restoration) this must have seemed a very old-fashioned case at the time it was made, especially to anyone who had seen the elaborately decorated rococo organ cases then being created for churches in Bavaria and Austria.

As ever, it was Renatus Harris who foresaw the trend and in his chair case at Salisbury in 1710 the two 'flat' compartments between the towers are curved in elevation and in plan. This led to the one British case design that perhaps does reflect a little of the rococo style. It was clearly made by a professional cabinetmaker (whose identity remains uncertain) and sold to all the leading organbuilders of the first half of the eighteenth century. Most were installed in the London area and, perhaps because of their outstanding quality as furniture, nearly all have survived. The distinguishing feature of these cases, apart from the uniformly high quality of carving and finish, is the ogee form, both in elevation and in plan, of the two 'flat' compartments between the towers. The workmanship involved in making the cornice members above these compartments attracts admiration from all who examine them. The only serious criticism is that, with single-storey flats, the smaller pipes have significant over-length, making them look etiolated and false. Decoration is beginning to triumph over honesty.

We do not know who designed these cases. The first one (in 1723 for St George, Botolph Lane, City of London) was on an organ by Abraham Jordan. The Botolph Lane case was moved, minus its casework below the impost, to the new church of St George, Southall, Middlesex, in 1908. It is in oak. Nearly all the later cases are in the then newly fashionable mahogany. They can be found in the following churches:

- St Paul, Deptford (Richard Bridge, 1730). Damaged by fire but recently restored with a new instrument by William Drake inside.
- St Vedast, Foster Lane (Harris and Byfield, 1732). In oak, built for St Bartholomew-by-the-Exchange, moved three times and installed in St Vedast in 1962.
- St John, Smith Square (Jordan, Byfield and Bridge, 1733). Built for St George, Great Yarmouth, Norfolk; modified in 1993 and a chair case added, all to house a very much bigger organ by Klais.
- Christ Church, Spitalfields (Richard Bridge, 1735). Largely in walnut, the curious diagonal upper cornices are not original. Currently awaiting restoration.
- St Helen, Bishopsgate (Thomas Griffin, 1744). Restored to its original west-gallery position in 1995.
- St Margaret Pattens, Rood Lane (Thomas Griffin, 1749). In its original position.
- St Andrew, Enfield, Middlesex (Richard Bridge, 1753). Moved to the front of the gallery with lower panelling removed.

The second half of the eighteenth century was not a good period for the Church of England, the main source of business. Organbuilders

St Margaret Pattens, City of London: case possibly made by Giles Grendey, organ by Thomas Griffin, 1749. (Drawing by Herbert Norman)

Cabinet by William Hallett, 1744. (Lady Lever Gallery, Port Sunlight)

Queen Anne and Georgian   45

concentrated instead on making chamber organs for the music rooms of the newly wealthy. Many have beautifully carved cases and have survived in village churches. One of the finest instruments was that constructed for the town house of Sir Watkin Williams Wynn, in St James's Square, London, with a case designed by Robert Adam. It is perhaps one of the first instances in this country of the organ being an ornament first and a musical instrument second. Adam picked up the circular pipe-display that Harris had used and introduced the use of mock drapery as pipe-shades.

As part of the general reining back in church work, relatively few new case designs were produced and many cases were made to simplified versions of older designs. As early as 1754 Richard Bridge had made, for Woolwich Parish Church, a three-tower case of similar proportions to those listed above but with flats which were straight, not ogee, on plan and with plain horizontal tip-boards. This case travelled to Fulton, Missouri, after World War Two, along with the rebuilt Church of St Mary Aldermanbury, City of London. In Rotherhithe, London, St Mary's Church has a grander version

Residence of Sir Watkin Williams Wynn, 20 St James's Square, London: case designed by Robert Adam, organ by John Snetzler, 1775. Now in the National Museum of Wales, Cardiff.

St Mary, Rotherhithe, London: John Byfield II, 1764.
(Photo: William McVicker)

46   The Box of Whistles

St Mary Magdalene, Richmond, Surrey: Thomas Knight, 1770.

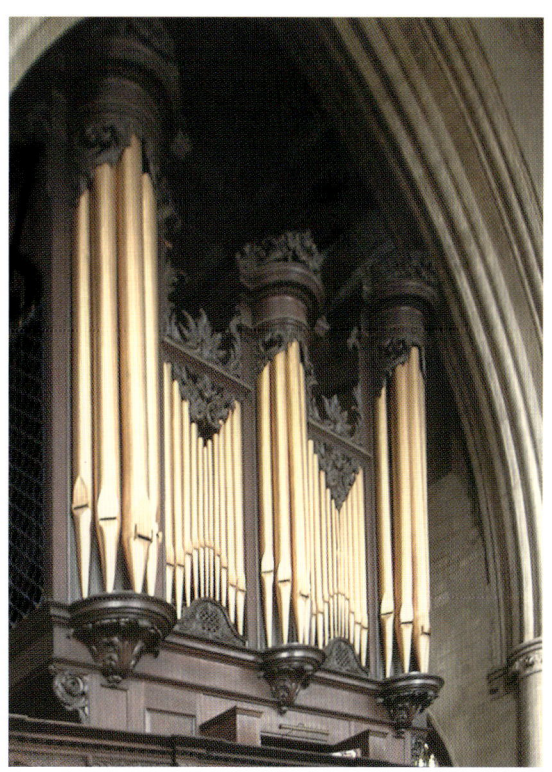

St Margaret, Kings Lynn: John Snetzler, 1754. (Photo: Edmund Holmes)

St Thomas, Ardwick, Manchester: Samuel Green, 1787. Now in St Paul, Salford. (Drawing by Herbert Norman)

of the same thing with good rococo carving (even if some is plaster not wood). The organ was built by John Byfield II (son) in 1764, possibly as a speculation, as the interior was altered before installation. The case is clearly of the same basic form as the London cases described above, the flats retaining the ogee tipboard shape in elevation but simplified to be straight on plan. The Thomas Knight case in St Mary Magdalene, Richmond, Surrey, is an elegant simplification of the same general style with less carving. It was to recur again in 1787 when Samuel Green reversed the tower heights for his instrument in St Thomas, Ardwick, Manchester.

John Snetzler was born in Switzerland and trained in southern Germany, coming to England

Queen Anne and Georgian 47

Peterhouse Chapel, Cambridge:
John Snetzler, 1765.

St Stephen, Walbrook, City of London:
George England, 1765.

about 1742. At first he made small chamber organs but in 1754 built a substantial organ for St Margaret's Church, Kings Lynn. He brought chamber organ standards of case finish to his church work and, although the impost is plain, there is much cresting above the tower caps and cornices. The Kings Lynn case demonstrates Snetzler's particular trademark of reversed panels of pipes in the flat compartments between the towers. He also, surprisingly, returned to a 'waisted' case with side overhangs. Recently restored, the front of this case survives at Kings Lynn, turned sideways in the north arcade instead of its original free-standing position on a screen across the church. Snetzler's 1765 case in the chapel of Peterhouse, Cambridge, is to a slightly different pattern, with a tall central tower and two-storey flats, the lower storey with Snetzler's trademark layout. Many Snetzler chamber organs remain intact, some in very fancy cases indeed (see page 112).

One of Snetzler's rivals was George England, who had worked with Richard Bridge and was his son-in-law. His finest case was that made for St Stephen, Walbrook, City of London, in 1765. He used Snetzler's device of reversed panels for the lower-storey flats, neatly combined with Harris-type oval panels for the upper storey. This case still stands at the west end of the church, with nineteenth-century Hill front pipes and slightly forward of its original position.

George England's nephew, George Pyke England, used a surprisingly similar design for his organ in Blandford Forum Parish Church, save that the outer towers are rectangular and flat instead of semicircular. Made in 1794, nearly

*Blandford Forum Parish Church:
George Pyke England, 1794. (Photo: Frances Moule)*

30 years later, it shows how much the development of case styles had slowed down.

At the chapel of the Royal Hospital, Greenwich, now known as the Old Naval College, the combination of an oval panel and Snetzler's reversed panel forms the central compartment of a four-tower case, unusual in having the middle towers subsidiary to the outer ones. This instrument was built in 1789 by Samuel Green, Snetzler's successor as organbuilder to the king.

One area in which styles did begin to change, however, was in the form of the pipe-shades. Usually foliate up to this date, a number of cases were made in which they took the form of imitation drapery, following Robert Adam's example in his organ for Sir Watkin Williams Wynn. However, the difficulty with this fashion is that the drapery cannot easily follow the pipe lengths, requiring obvious false length on the smaller pipes in order to fill the space revealed. This shows in the case of the 1791 Samuel Green

*Chapel of the Royal Hospital, Greenwich:
Samuel Green, 1789.*

organ in St Botolph's Church, Aldersgate, City of London. Here Green went up to five towers, with two subsidiary towers nestling against the sides of the wide central tower. The Aldersgate case also shows Adam influence in the delicate carving of the details. The use of a contrasting wood for the panel mouldings is very unusual in organ cases.

The 1792 George Pyke England case at St James, Clerkenwell, London, is original in having palm fronds above the cornices instead of the figure-work which had been traditional 100 years before. The pipe-shade problem is handled quite cleverly in the lower flats, the swags hanging down at the sides to more or less

Queen Anne and Georgian 49

*St Botolph, Aldersgate,
City of London:
Samuel Green, 1791*

*St James, Clerkenwell, London: George Pyke England,
1792. (Drawing by Herbert Norman)*

*St Mary, Stafford: John Geib, 1790.
(Drawing by Herbert Norman)*

50   The Box of Whistles

Cabinet cresting based on a Chippendale design, 1754. (Lady Lever Gallery, Port Sunlight)

follow the pipe lengths. The pipe-length problem became even worse with the later fashion for Grecian-style cases (see page 55). With no pipe-shades and all pipes the same length whatever their diameter, the front pipes then looked for all the world like fluting on a column.

John Geib, of German descent, combined organbuilding and piano-making in Britain before moving to New York (where one of his pianos is in the Metropolitan Museum of Art). His one surviving case here, in St Mary, Stafford, dating from 1790, is notable for its two-storey central tower and overall double-storey structure. This case had been reduced to a mere screen but was restored to its original free-standing position in the west end of the church in 1974. Geib used almost exactly the same design in 1802, 12 years later, for St Paul's Chapel, Manhattan, near the site today of the destroyed World Trade Center towers. This case also survives, widened with additional towers either side.

The big new idea in architecture in the late eighteenth century was a return to Gothic. As initially practised, it was merely a new style of ornament, applied without an understanding of the structural rationale that lay behind it. The earliest surviving Gothic Revival organ case,

The inspiration for the spires at Dulwich? Palma Cathedral, Majorca, fifteenth century. (From a drawing by A. G. Hill)

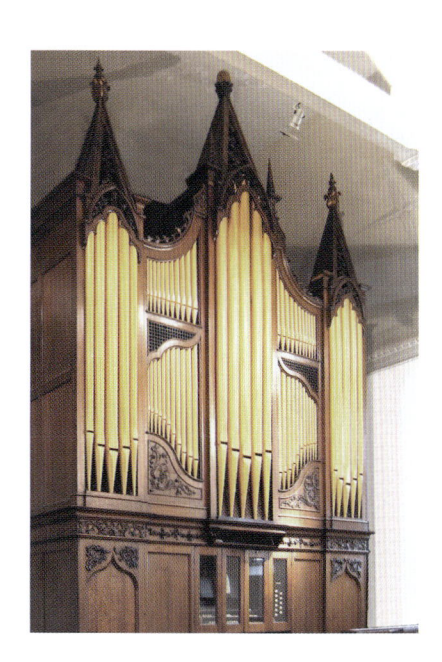

The earliest surviving Gothic Revival organ case, Christ's Chapel, Dulwich, London: George England, 1760. (Photo: William McVicker)

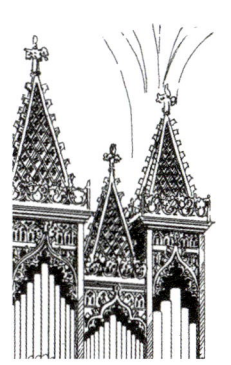

Exeter Cathedral: the spires were added in the eighteenth century and removed in nineteenth century. (Detail from a contemporary engraving by John Pearce)

Queen Anne and Georgian 51

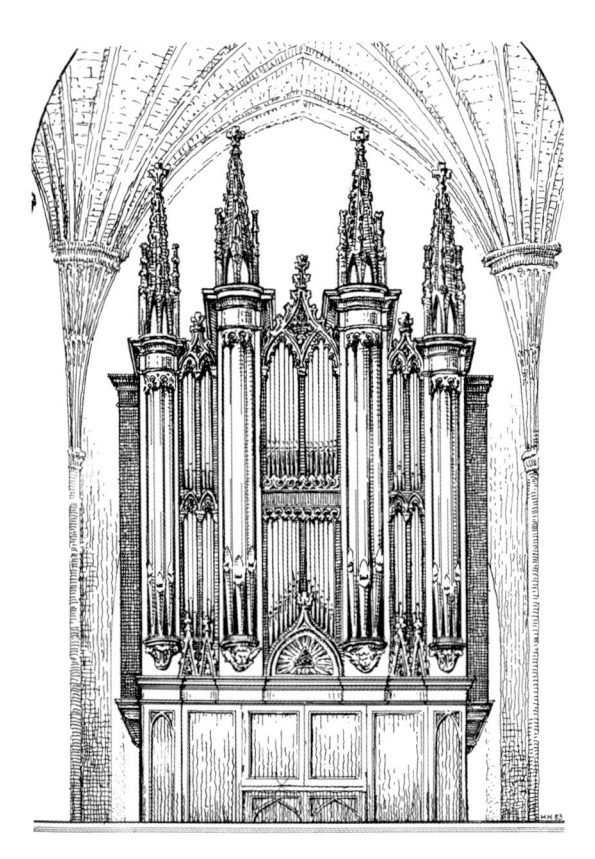

Wymondham Abbey, Norfolk: James Davis, 1794.
(Drawing by Herbert Norman)

St Mary the Virgin, Oxford: Bernard Smith, 1675,
Gothicized by Thomas Plowman in 1827.
Now in St Mary the Virgin, Penzance.
(Photo: Andrew Freeman/British Organ Archive)

dating from 1760, is by George England, in Christ's Chapel, Dulwich. Like much other early Gothic Revival furniture inspired by Batty Langley, the Gothic decoration is rather superficially applied. Nevertheless, the three spires are distinctive and unusual and may have been based on a fifteenth-century original in Palma, Majorca.

Spires seem to have been associated with the early Gothic Revival as far as organs are concerned. One of the sillier ideas of the late eighteenth century was the addition of spires to the tower caps of the seventeenth-century organ cases in Exeter and Gloucester cathedrals and King's College Chapel, Cambridge. Not surprisingly, none have survived.

One example of a really confused organ case is in Wymondham Abbey, Norfolk, built by James Davis in 1794. The fundamental structure is based on the classic Father Smith four-tower design, with semicircular towers supported on cherubs' heads. The towers, however, have only three pipes each instead of the usual five, giving them a tall thin appearance; above the tower caps stand four beautifully crocketed Gothic spires. The three two-storey flats are each divided into two sub-compartments by thin mullions joined at the top by Gothic arches, the upper storey terminating in curved gables. So we have eighteenth-century Gothic decoration

52   The Box of Whistles

added to a Renaissance substratum on a basically medieval Gothic structure! Yet, despite it all, well situated in its original position on the west gallery of this splendid building, the case actually looks very grand. Smith's four-tower design also lived on, simplified and without Gothic decoration, in George Pyke England's 1814 instrument in St Mary Magdalene, Islington, London, and was to get another airing later in the century, as we shall see.

One case showing mixed styles, now removed to St Mary's Church, Penzance, was the 1675 Father Smith case in St Mary the Virgin, Oxford, which was gothicized by the architect Thomas Plowman in 1827. Smith's basic three-tower case with two-storey flats retained its original shape but was stripped of most of its original ornament and the tower caps, cornices and pipe-shades replaced.

One of the last big nineteenth-century cases to be designed by an organbuilder was built by Henry Lincoln in 1821 for St John's Chapel, Bedford Row, London. Now in the glorious medieval Thaxted Parish Church, Essex, it contains a mixture of Gothic and Renaissance decoration.

After 1820, architects became involved with nearly all the important organ cases. E. J. Willson designed the case for William Allen's 1826 organ at Lincoln Cathedral. The basic structure of the main case is still the Smith/Harris recipe of three towers and two flats, though the flats run up to Gothic arches and the tops of the towers support intricate spirelets, leading to the term 'prickly Gothic'. On the east side there is a chair case which is

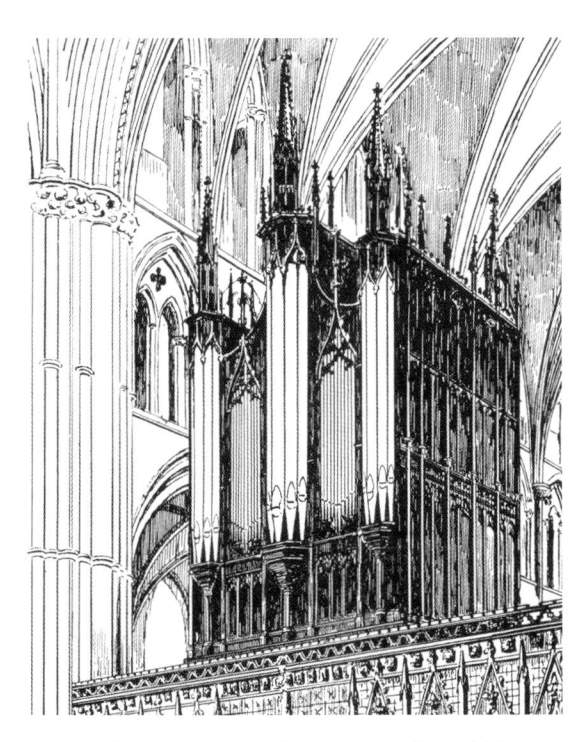

Lincoln Cathedral (west face): E. J. Willson, 1826. The case was made taller by J. L. Pearson in 1898. Organs by William Allen, 1826, and Henry Willis, 1898. (Drawing by H. T. Lilley)

Winchester Cathedral: Edward Blore, 1825. (Photo: Gilbert Benham)

St Matthew, Birmingham: Anon., c.1830. Now in Carey Baptist Church, Hemel Hempstead, Hertfordshire.

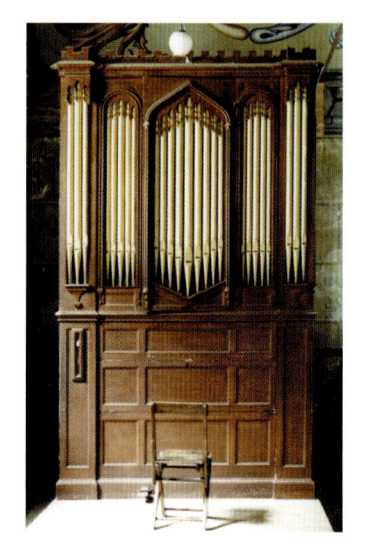

São Vicente Church, Madeira: Flight & Robson, 'Organbuilders to the Prince Regent'.

more original, and looks interesting on plan, perhaps taking after Jutphaas (see page 16), though much less interesting in practice with its almost flat top and five equal panels of front pipes.

Another architect-designed case of similar date shows very clearly a problem that was to rear its ugly head time and time again. The case front at Winchester Cathedral, designed by Edward Blore to replace a seventeenth-century four-tower case by Thomas Thamer, is no longer part of the organ but a pure screen erected in front of the instrument. The pipe-caps at the tops of the towers have become two-dimensional spires and, as the design scheme did not include any flats, the spaces between the three main towers are filled with two narrow towers, containing unnaturally etiolated pipes plus some slightly awkward single-pipe compartments, the latter a feature which was to crop up again at York Minster.

The softwood case made *c.*1830 for St Matthew, Birmingham (now in Carey Baptist Church, Hemel Hempstead) is a more typical early Gothic Revival case for an ordinary church. It is a complete change from the towers and flats

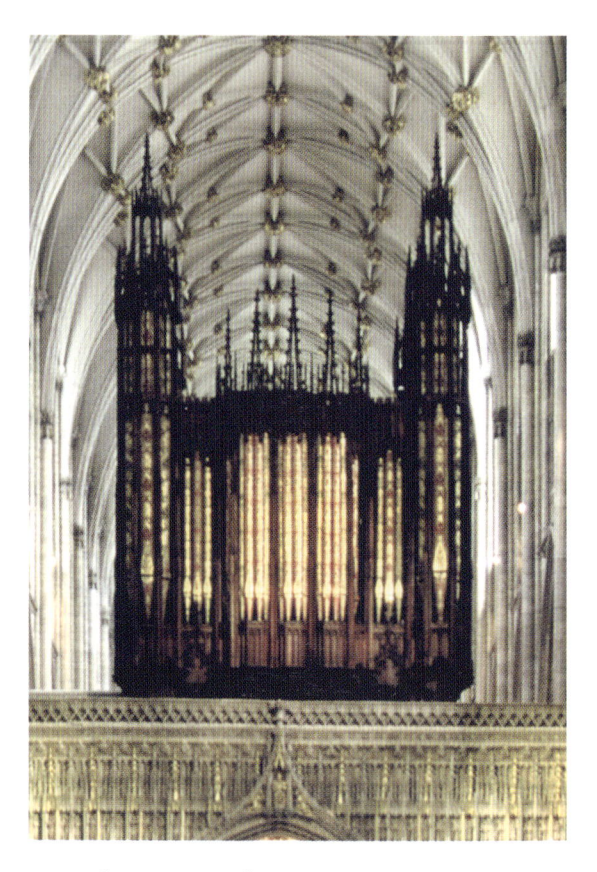

York Minster (west face): Sir Robert Smirke, 1829. Organ by Elliot & Hill. (Photo: Duncan Booth)

54   The Box of Whistles

St John, Waterloo Road, Lambeth, London: Francis Bedford, 1824. Organ by J. C. Bishop. Modified by Noel Mander, 1951.

St James, Bermondsey, London: James Savage, 1829. Organ by J. C. Bishop.

which had been characteristic of organ cases since medieval beginnings. Flat-fronted, the centre is occupied by a wide seven-pipe compartment with an arched and gabled top, flanked by two compartments each side of different scale, surmounted by large-scale Gothic pipe-shades and a castellated cornice.

The case at York Minster is a still more original design. Made for the very large 1829 Elliot & Hill organ, the largest in the country at the time, it was designed by Sir Robert Smirke. The main body of the case has angled corners on an almost rectangular structure, within which narrow 'windows' of front pipes are each surmounted by Gothic pinnacles and a spirelet. The relatively narrow towers at each corner are divided into single-pipe compartments, with the tops of the bass pipes disappearing into a gradually increasing mass of arches, tabernacles and pinnacles. The end result is a huge Gothic tabernacle, of slightly dumpy proportions, in which the front pipes have become incidental to the overall design.

For those who did not like Gothic Revival, the 1820s were the heyday of the Greek Classical style in architecture. Churches were built with columns and pedimented porticos – a style which, these days, we think of as 'Banker's Georgian'. Without any ancient Greek organ cases to use as models, attempts were made to make the organs themselves look like Greek temples. John Nash tried this in 1824 at All Souls, Langham Place, London with a thin pediment over a central tower 17 pipes wide,

Queen Anne and Georgian   55

no pipe-shades and with front pipes nearly all the same length. In the same year, Francis Bedford made the pediment run the full width of the main case at St John's, Lambeth. This design is more successful, especially as it was originally provided with pipe-shades (mostly removed in 1951).

At St James, Bermondsey, James Savage did not attempt to make the organ mimic his Greek Classical church. The 1829 case of this otherwise fine organ looks as much like an oversize monument as it does the housing for an organ. The pipe compartments appear as windows in a solid and top-heavy structure. The rudimentary pipe-shades, in the form of mock drapery, do nothing for the front pipes. As at York Minster and Langham Place, many of the pipes appear all to be sounding the same note!

Sadly, the Georgian period, which had started so well, moved first to stagnation and then to near fantasy. At first the succeeding years did little better.

6
BACK TO BASICS?

The reign of Queen Victoria, and the years immediately before, found organ case design totally without direction. Organbuilders had few fresh ideas. The case of William Hill's 1834 organ for Birmingham Town Hall is a giant version of the Father Smith three-tower design, scaled up to accommodate 32 ft front pipes instead of 10 ft and enlarged by the addition of two more towers, set back at the sides. The photograph shows the case before some alterations *c.*1927 but includes the 1890 front pipe decoration.

William Hill's 1848 organ in St Mary-at-Hill, City of London, also went back to Smith for its inspiration, this time using his four-tower design, scaled up to use 16 ft front pipes. The design only fell down in the side flats, where all the pipes appear to be the same length. This case has recently been repaired and restored, following a disastrous fire in 1986.

Another example, of the same date and only a short distance away, is the case of the T. C. Bates organ in St Martin, Ludgate Hill,

Birmingham Town Hall (before alterations c.1927): William Hill, 1834. (Photo: Hill Norman & Beard)

St Mary-at-Hill, Lovat Lane, City of London: William Hill, 1848. (Photo: Mander Organs)

Back to basics? 57

*St Martin, Ludgate Hill, City of London:
Theodore Bates, 1848.*

*The Great Exhibition, 1851: attributed to Albert Howell.
Organ by Gray & Davison.
Installed in St Anne, Limehouse, London.*

just below St Paul's Cathedral. Here the classic late sixteenth-century three-tower design was the inspiration, although in a debased form with minimal pipe-shade carving; all the tower pipes are apparently the same length and the pipes in the flats are very narrow.

Architects were also uncertain about case design. Gilbert Scott, in one of his first important commissions, at St Giles, Camberwell, London, even ducked out of providing a case at all for J. C. Bishop's 1844 organ, hiding it behind an openwork screen. But the direction of ecclesiastical architecture was changing. From about 1840, architects started to tire of 'secular' Georgian and of 'unscholarly Gothick' and searched for the real medieval Gothic. With virtually no medieval Gothic organ cases to copy in Britain, many designers sought a lead from the style of the medieval portative organ, as depicted in the Van Eyck triptych (see page 1). They felt that medieval simplicity was best expressed in an organ case which consisted only of bass pipes plus any necessary supports.

In a sense they were right. The organ case had long lost some of the functional reasons for its existence. No longer was it an ornamental box, needed to keep out dust and vandals; few British organ cases had been made with roofs for some time and, other than for some chamber organs, doors had disappeared before 1600. The Gray & Davison organ now in St Anne, Limehouse, London, was built for the Great Exhibition of 1851. The case, attributed to Albert Howell, dispenses with nearly all the woodwork above impost level. Only the towers have pipe-caps,

58   The Box of Whistles

St George's Hall, Liverpool: Christopher Cockerell, 1855. Organ by Henry Willis.

Detail of crowns on tops of bass pipes.

Upton Scudamore Parish Church, Wiltshire. (Drawing by G. E. Street, from John Baron, Scudamore Organs, *1858)*

and insubstantial ones at that. The tops of the front pipes (most of which have substantial overlength to make them tall enough to conceal the interior) are exposed above a visible pipe-stay. This was the way the Victorians wanted to go in the age of steam: simple and apparently functional. Few real organ cases would be made for several decades.

This did not stop inventive architects from adding decoration to the new style. Christopher Cockerell's design for the 1855 Willis concert organ in St George's Hall, Liverpool, shows great panache in its handling of bass pipes, importing all manner of decorative ideas. Notice how, as at Limehouse, the architect blenched at leaving the tallest pipes uncovered, covering them with applied crowns.

It fell to the Revd John Baron to express the idea of the medieval portative in a church organ. His influential book espoused simplicity. The appearance of the small organ in his village church was, in effect, the Van Eyck triptych instrument writ large. One early implementer was the then young J. L. Pearson in his remarkable church at Daylesford in the Cotswolds. Others would go on to develop this idea and, in doing so, be even more cavalier with scale.

After 1844 Gilbert Scott recovered his confidence in case design and at Ely Cathedral in 1851 adopted the medieval case in Strasbourg Cathedral as his model. The cantilevered structure was then unique in Britain but, of the detail, only the chair case outline actually came from Strasbourg. In 1854 Scott went overboard for naked pipe-tops at King's College, London, but also for very fine figure-painting on the pipes and the use of a lacy metal pipe-stay – less dominant than a wood one. He reverted to ornamenting the tops of the largest pipes in his giant 32 ft case for the transept of Worcester Cathedral (1874). This is a relatively conventional three-tower design, possibly

St Peter, Daylesford, Gloucestershire: J. L. Pearson, 1864. Organ by John Nicholson. The front pipes are reversed, treble to bass, to avoid conflict with the rose window.

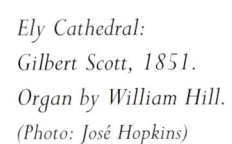

Ely Cathedral: Gilbert Scott, 1851. Organ by William Hill. (Photo: José Hopkins)

Strasbourg Cathedral: Friedrich Krebs, 1489.

60   The Box of Whistles

King's College Chapel, Strand, London: Gilbert Scott, 1854. Organ by Henry Willis. Lower casework removed in 1932.

Worcester Cathedral, transept: Gilbert Scott, 1874. Organ by Hill & Son.

influenced by Thomas Hill the organbuilder, with a thin two-storey central tower terminating in a delicately ornamented spire. However, the 32 ft bass pipes in the wide side towers rise up through the cornice of the upper pipe-caps and terminate in ornamental crowns. Each tower has an inverted and crocketted spire pendant below it. This may be a medley of Gothic features but it is certainly not Gothic as our medieval forebears knew it.

Another factor entered the equation in the second half of the nineteenth century. It had long been customary for organs to be placed on galleries at the west end of churches. The amateur choirs were considered relatively unimportant and were accommodated on the gallery in front of the organ, out of sight of the congregation but conveniently close to the organist. In cathedrals, boys and professional singers occupied stalls in the Choir originally provided for monks before the Reformation. However, after 1845, there was a widespread movement in the Church of England to copy the cathedral pattern and dress parish choirs up

Back to basics?

in surplices and to place them in choir stalls between the altar and the congregation. The practical difficulties of accompanying an east-end choir from a west-end organ forced almost every parish church either to move or replace their organ over the succeeding 30 years.

But where were the organs to go? Larger churches had sizeable transepts but most had to cram the organs into east-end chapels, side aisles, or specially constructed organ chambers on one side of the chancel (preferably the north side, where the organ receives less heat in summer and thus the tuning is more stable). This had musical effects which do not concern us here (the organs had to be larger and more powerful to overcome the less favourable sound egress). It did, however, mean that the majority of new organs were no longer free-standing pieces of furniture but were tailored into organ chambers or other recesses in the building structure. The case was thus reduced to a fence of bass pipes hiding the interior. With the organ tucked away into a low aisle or organ chamber, any structure above the pipe-tops would obstruct the egress of sound, and woodwork other than a simple post-and-rail pipe support was eschewed. Because of the numbers of new churches built in the second half of the nineteenth century, large numbers of organs were built in this style, many of which are still in use and, to many people, this is the general image of what an organ looks like.

The 1880 Hill organ in St John's Church, Stamford, Lincolnshire, can be taken as an example for thousands of others. Above softwood panelling, there is a simple row of bass pipes, grouped as if arranged in three compartments. The foot lengths are an odd mixture, those at the sides having conventional shorter feet on the longer pipes so that the line of the pipe-mouths is said to smile. The larger centre panel reverses this to have the longest foot on the longest pipe, presumably to lift the tops of the centre pipes to conceal as much as

St John, Stamford, Lincolnshire: Hill & Son, 1880.

possible of the works behind. The pipe-stay supporting the front pipes is decorated with drilled quatrefoils, carved brackets and pinnacled posts with poppyheads. The bass pipes were originally covered in stencilled coloured decoration.

The organbuilder 'Father' Henry Willis notoriously grudged spending money on casework. His 1876 organ for Durham Cathedral has a relatively minimal pipe-stay, supported by almost invisible iron uprights. The next year, in his musically very successful organ for Salisbury Cathedral, and at the suggestion of the architect G. E. Street, Willis fitted loops on the backs of the front pipes so that they could be held by hooks fitted to the 'half-moon' stays behind the

Salisbury Cathedral: Henry Willis, 1877.

St Augustine, Penarth, Cardiff: Hill & Son, 1895.

pipes. This meant that the pipes were entirely supported from behind, with no visible stay in front of them. Although the pipes are still arranged in towers and flats, the appearance of the organ was further simplified, consisting only of lower panelling and the front pipes themselves, their plain zinc finish trying to melt into the similarly dimensioned Purbeck marble shafts of the arcade behind them. This style was to become much more prevalent in the years after 1900.

The idea of the bare pipe-top became so ingrained that, even where a case-front was attempted, it became quite usual to have the bass pipes sticking up over the pipe-caps. The 1895 case at St Augustine, Penarth, is the Hill version of a style that became very common in the 1880–1900 period. There was reputedly a double standard in the Hill firm at this time; if the client was prepared to pay for a grand case, Dr Arthur Hill would design it personally. If not, you got a stock design like Penarth, worked up by the case-shop foreman.

7
THE REAL GOTHIC REVIVAL

Despite the mediocrity which characterizes the cases of most instruments built in the second half of the nineteenth century, there are a few which rise above the others, mostly designed by a select few enlightened architects who had taken the trouble to inform themselves about medieval Gothic cases surviving on the Continent. A. W. N. Pugin was the enthusiastic champion of medieval Gothic architecture who turned his attention to organs at the behest of the wealthy and talented Sir John Sutton. The one organ case generally credited to Pugin and constructed in his lifetime is the quite small instrument in the chapel of Jesus College, Cambridge. This was paid for by Sutton and recent scholarship suggests that Sutton sketched the basic design which was then worked up by Pugin. The case is fully roofed and waisted but, as is typical of creative minds, it is a fresh combination of early sixteenth-century ideas rather than a slavish copy of a medieval original. Without outer towers outside the two flats, it is saved from weakness at the corners by the strongly angular folding doors.

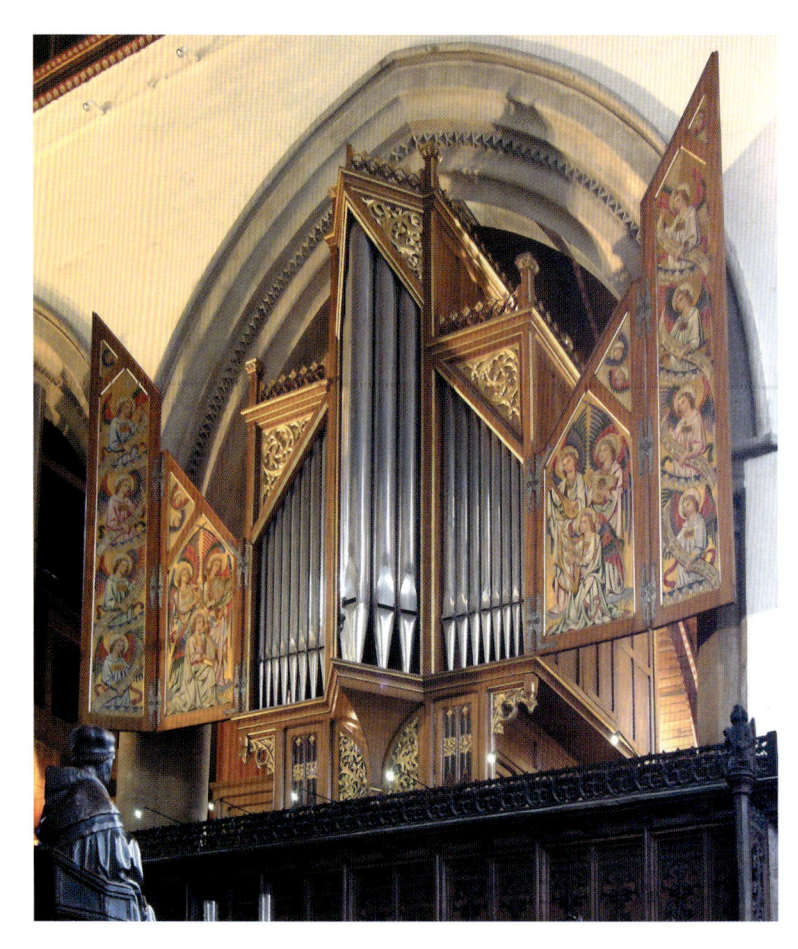

Jesus College Chapel, Cambridge:
Sir John Sutton/A. W. N. Pugin, 1849. Organ by J. C. Bishop.

A simpler case, in the same idiom, can be found in the Church of St Mary the Virgin, Great Bardfield in Essex. It is thought that the case of the A. T. Miller organ of *c.*1860 was designed by the Revd F. H. Sutton, Sir John's brother. Here there is no actual tower but the flat front is divided into three compartments and carved wings are substituted for doors.

A much less 'correct' but much more individual case was that designed by R. C. Carpenter for the 1856 Gray & Davison organ in Sherborne Abbey. He resurrected the chair case, giving it a simple outline, not entirely unlike Pugin's Jesus College case. He included vestigial doors in the form of fixed Gothic tracery and a small amount of 'waisting' below the impost. The upper part of the case, however, is a totally original composition. The case has a practical fault in that the richly

St Mary the Virgin, Great Bardfield, Essex. Attributed to F. H. Sutton, c.1860, organ by A. T. Miller. (Photo: Michael Young)

Sherborne Abbey, Dorset: R. C. Carpenter, 1856. Organ by Gray & Davison.

Sherborne Abbey, detail of chair case and soffit.

The real Gothic revival   65

decorated front pipes are packed too close together, almost touching, restricting the egress of sound.

It was some time before these pioneering efforts bore fruit; the appearance of the vast majority of organs built at this time was much like the Stamford instrument illustrated in the last chapter (see page 62). Some otherwise respected Victorian church architects, S. S. Teulon and Ewan Christian for example, designed disastrous organ fronts. In the last quarter of the century, however, certain architects emerged with a better understanding of case design, and were mostly employed by the more ambitious churches.

One of these was the Church of St Bartholomew, Armley, Leeds, designed by the local firm of Walker & Athron. Their work included the massive and exuberant American walnut case for the organ, given by a single donor in 1879 to house an organ by the influential German organbuilder Edmund Schulze. The design is quite original, with a basic three-tower structure augmented by side wings and pediment-like sloping side supports to the main central tower. The three-pipe side towers return round the corner to reduce the apparent projection of the instrument, a device later copied by others. The chief criticism of this case is the huge differential in scale between the

St Bartholomew, Armley, Leeds: Walker & Athron, 1879.
Organ by Edmund Schulze, Paulinzella, Thuringia.

*Eton College Chapel:
J. L. Pearson, 1882.
Organ by Hill & Son.*

pipes in the 16 ft towers and those in the flat compartments. The tower pipes are so fat that the largest has no musical use and had to be a dummy. The strange gilded bands round the pipes may have been a practical device to hide the joins in the zinc pipes.

J. L. Pearson went from his early 'pipe-rack' at Daylesford to the quite remarkable case for the 1882 Hill organ in Eton College Chapel. This is a double-sided case which seems to grow out of the Gothic Revival screen on which it stands. The east face is remarkable for the bold use of circular towers with minimal intervening flats; a central group of three 8 ft towers is flanked by 16 ft towers, flanked in their turn by 32 ft towers. This variety of scale, assisted by the small chair case, helps to avoid the 32 ft pipes becoming overwhelming. The round-topped 'French' pipe-mouths were virtually standard on Hill organs; the painted decoration on these pipes is some of the best the nineteenth century ever produced (see the photograph on page 9).

The real Gothic revival 67

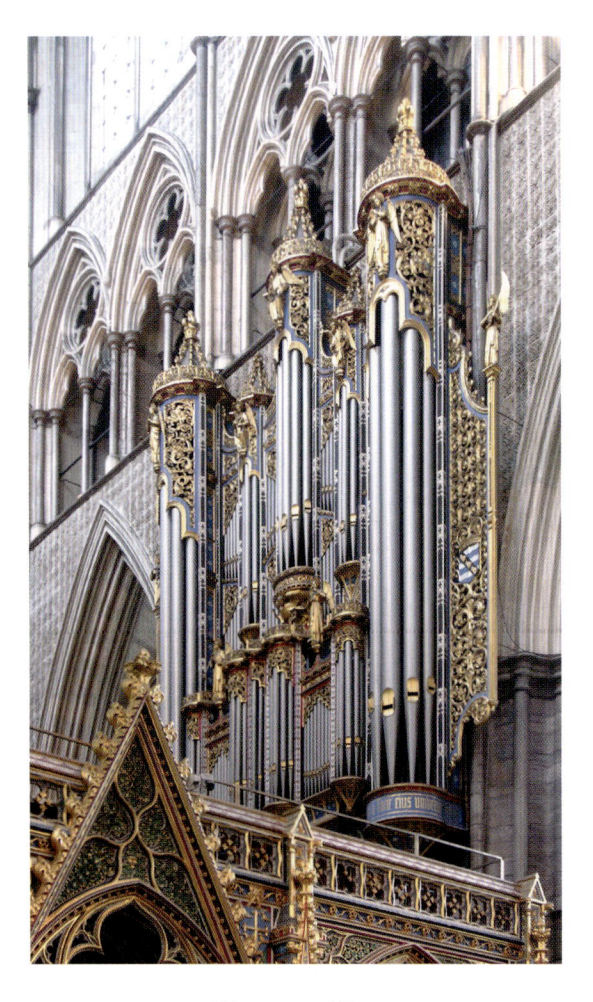

Westminster Abbey:
J. L. Pearson, 1896–9. Organ by Hill & Son.

Pearson produced a number of designs for cases that were never completed, notably Truro Cathedral, where space for the uprights was left between the front pipes but the posts, caps and cornices never inserted. At Brisbane Cathedral, Pearson put the organ in his favourite north-side position, forgetting that, in Australia, the sun goes round the other way. Here, one case was completed but not the other. Pearson's twin cases for Westminster Abbey, completed in 1899, were in some respects more conventional but contain a wide variety of tower shapes

Westminster Abbey, detail of case painting: Stephen Dykes-Bower, 1959.

(semicircular, V-shaped and flat) as well as a variety of pipe sizes. Each case is subtly different, with a shallow mock chair case on each side and back cases facing into the aisles. The Abbey cases were dismantled when the organ was rebuilt in 1937 but restored in 1959, when they received their present superb painted decoration at the hands of Stephen Dykes-Bower. The lining of the edges of the uprights, augmented with little Gothic arches, is remarkably effective.

A. G. Hill (later Dr Hill) also started to make his mark in the 1880s. Although briefly in Scott's office, he was not an architect but an organbuilder, grandson of William Hill. He had a natural design talent, shown by *The Organ-cases and Organs of the Middle Ages and Renaissance*, published in two parts in 1883 (when he was but 26) and in 1891. These were influential

Chichester Cathedral, front pipe detail.

Chichester Cathedral: A. G. Hill, 1888. Organ by Hill & Son.

Peterborough Cathedral; A. G. Hill, 1904. Organ by Hill & Son, 1894. (Photo: Hill Norman & Beard)

(the subscription lists included many prominent church architects) and some of the illustrations are published in this volume. The soaring three-tower case for Chichester Cathedral (1888) attracted significant attention and, over the years, several imitations. Its distinctive silhouette includes bands of carving on the tower caps (later to become a feature of the work of G. F. Bodley). As befits an organbuilder, the proportions of all the front pipes are correct, without any hint of false length, even in the daring perspective-like lower flats. The chair case was Dr Hill's only essay in this medium; a distinctive and original design.

Like Pugin, Hill had the ability to take medieval structure and decoration and work them into a totally original conception. This is also shown in his case for Peterborough

The real Gothic revival 69

Bolton Parish Church: A. G. Hill, 1882. Organ rebuilt by Hill & Son.

cases were left in exposed oak, it shows his ability to provide strong colour when required.

Hill's last major case, at Beverley Minster (1916) was, in many ways, the end of an era. Perfectly balanced to the height of the nave, this is a three-tower case with a difference, the slender three-pipe side towers being matched by the lower-set central tower of similar dimensions but two storeys. The case is waisted out to support two side flats as well as the flats between the towers. This case is a good example

Cathedral (1904), where what appears at first to be the central flat becomes a central tower when one reaches the top of the case. Like Peterborough, Hill's case at Bolton Parish Church can be criticized for being purely a screen, without direct relationship to the layout of the organ behind it, but at a time when most

Beverley Minster: A. G. Hill, 1916–20. Organ rebuilt by Hill & Son. (Drawing by Herbert Norman)

St German, Roath, Cardiff: G. F. Bodley, 1885. Organ by Hill & Son.

70   The Box of Whistles

of the way organbuilders' cases have less wood in them than many architects' cases. Although looking solid from the outside it is actually quite lightly built and thus very transparent to sound.

G. F. Bodley and Hill must have been on good terms as they worked together on a number of cases for Hill's instruments. Bodley was keen on projecting organ cases forward on bold coving, generally with flat, non-projecting towers. His case at St German, Roath, Cardiff is a good example, with its clever use of two storeys. As in Hill's case at Peterborough, there is an interesting ambiguity over what are flats and what are towers.

At St Michael, Croydon, the towers project, but otherwise the case at first appears to be a

Paisley Abbey: Sir Robert Lorimer, 1928. (Photo: Hill Norman & Beard)

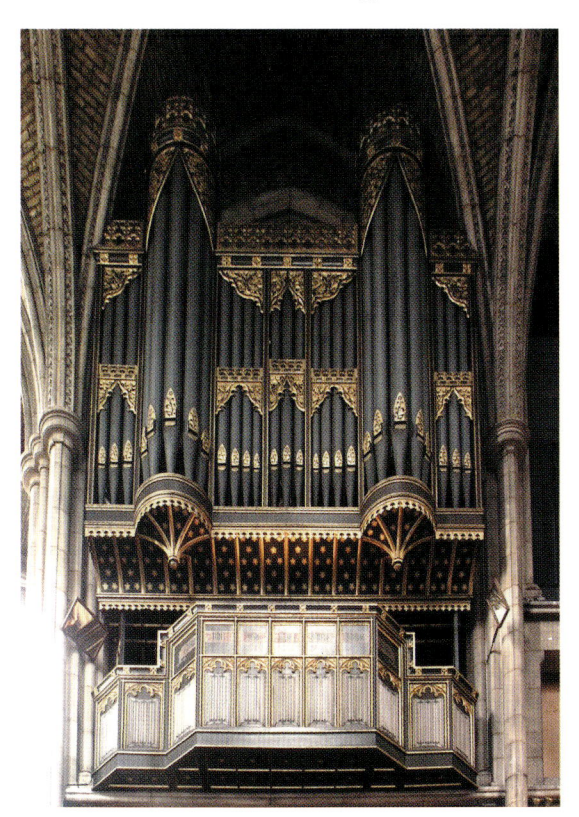

typical two-storey Bodley creation, with cove and cornice decoration. Unfortunately, however, Bodley had the misfortune to come up against Father Henry Willis as the organbuilder, very able but a notorious phobic where organ cases

St Michael, Croydon (chancel case): G. F. Bodley, completed 1909. Organ by Henry Willis. (Photo: William McVicker)

St Mary, Lavant, West Sussex: Sir Arthur Blomfield, 1895. Organ by Hill & Son.

The real Gothic revival

were concerned. The result was really only a single-storey case, with long pipes based in the lower storey running up and pretending to be part of the upper storey also.

Another designer who eschewed projecting towers was Sir Robert Lorimer. His ornately carved but rather boxy case at Paisley Abbey was designed earlier but not erected until 1928. Some of the front pipe foot-lengths ran the wrong way but were altered in 1968.

A further knighted architect, Sir Arthur Blomfield, was less successful at organ cases. Drawing a veil over his curious case in Southwark Cathedral, the more conventional case at St Mary, Lavant, Sussex, nevertheless exhibits a classic fault in placing front pipes in the tower return.

Gilbert Scott's son John Oldrid Scott designed very much more correct Gothic organ cases than his father. They were, in fact, rather dull. His best known is the pair of cases, side by side and dated 1889, in his father's chapel at St John's College, Cambridge. Here the lower part of each main case is screened by a wide mock chair case. The musically distinctive horizontal trumpet pipes peeping over the right-hand case were added in 1955.

Giles Gilbert Scott (later Sir Giles), grandson of Gilbert Scott, worked rather under the thumb of Bodley when he designed the lovely Lady

St John's College Chapel, Cambridge: J. Oldrid Scott, 1889. Trumpet pipes added in 1955. (Photo: Hill Norman & Beard)

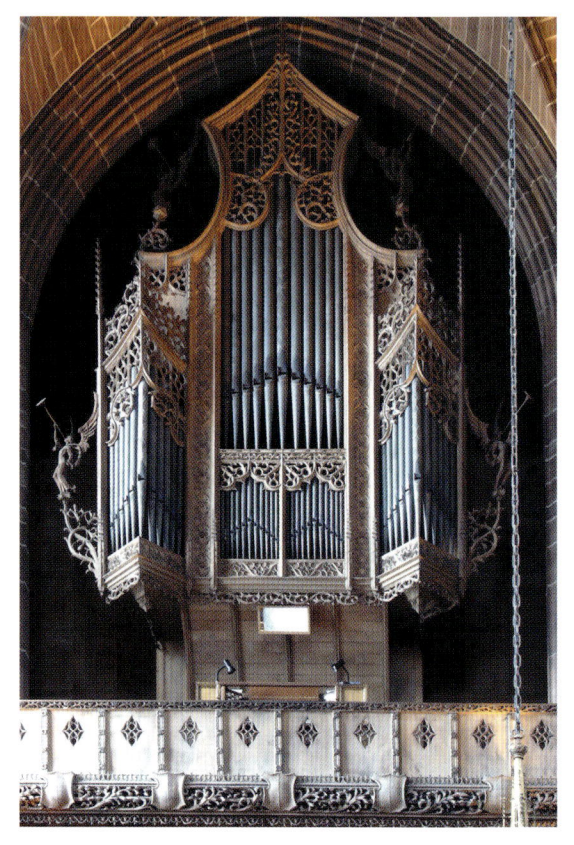

Liverpool Cathedral Lady Chapel: attributed to Giles Gilbert Scott, 1910. Organ by Henry Willis III.

Holy Trinity, Prince Consort Road, Kensington: Cecil Hare, 1911. Organ by Brindley & Foster.

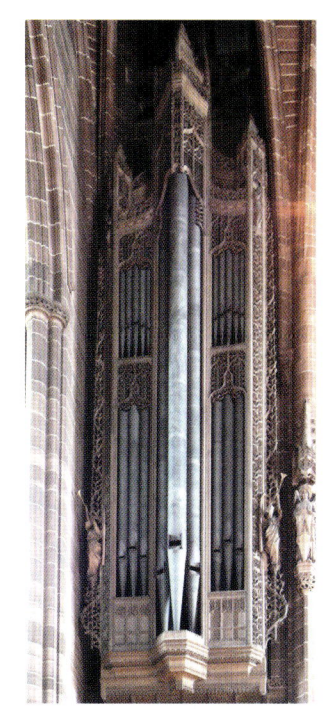

Liverpool Cathedral (crossing case): Giles Gilbert Scott, 1924. Organ by Henry Willis III.

Winchester College Chapel: W. D. Caroe, 1908. Organ by Norman & Beard. (Drawing by Herbert Norman)

Chapel at Liverpool Cathedral. The prominent coving under the impost suggests Bodley's ideas but the superstructure, with its short V-pointed side towers, is quite unlike his usual work. The central flat that runs up to form a bold and dramatic silhouette is a unique invention. It so happens that there is a medieval tomb in the crypt of a church in Venice with a similar outline; perhaps no coincidence, as it is known that Bodley travelled widely. The other feature is the striking similarity to the organ case in Holy Trinity Church, Prince Consort Road, Kensington, with similar pointed side towers. Designed by Cecil Hare, Bodley's partner, it was completed one year after the Liverpool case.

The real Gothic revival 73

Sadly, Scott's organ cases in the chancel at Liverpool Cathedral, designed later, after Bodley's death, are much less original and the 32 ft cases facing the crossing strangely etiolated.

Like the instrument in the Lady Chapel at Liverpool, the case of the 1908 organ in the chapel of Winchester College has a very original silhouette. W. D. Caroe combined Gothic elements in an innovative way, with a three-storey central tower and nearly separate round side towers which contrast with the rectangular outline of the central structure.

One detail common to the last two cases is the use of plain zinc for the front pipes, without paint or decoration. This was to become increasingly common as the twentieth century wore on. As noted earlier, zinc oxidizes to a dull matt grey surface, reducing the dominance of an oversize case, but otherwise lacking in visual appeal.

8
NOT ALL GOTHIC

The influence of the Gothic style was not, of course, all-pervasive. Thomas Lainson, architect of Reading Town Hall, designed an extraordinary organ case in Victorian Baroque to match the hall. The unconventional curved towers and massive caryatids either side of the console indicate a designer confident enough to take liberties with conventional forms and to get away with it.

Dr Hill was a more cautious designer, but his 1889 magnificent Renaissance-inspired 32 ft case for the organ in Sydney Town Hall, Australia, was in many ways his *magnum opus*. This instrument was then the largest organ in the world and still remains unaltered and in daily use. The case bears its large scale very lightly with the aid of some two-storey V-shape towers

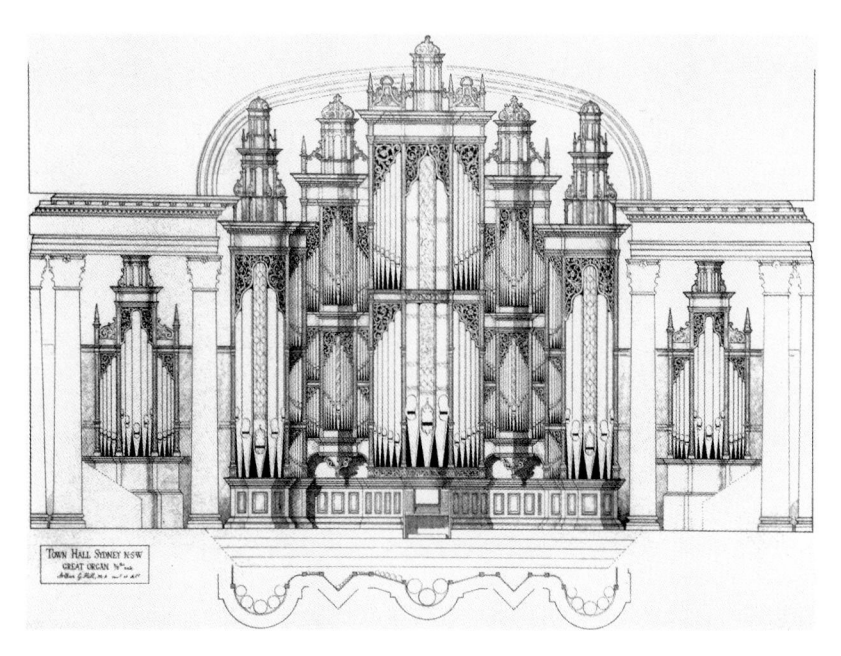

Reading Town Hall: Thomas Lainson, 1864. Organ by Henry Willis. (Drawing by Herbert Norman)

Sydney Town Hall, Australia: A. G. Hill, 1889. Organ by Hill & Son. (Drawing by A. G. Hill)

and three-storey flats. The mouth shapes on the three largest 32 ft pipes are noteworthy, as are the pavilions on top of the towers.

Philip Selfe, another organbuilder-designer, produced a much simpler case in 1911 for the City Hall in Hull. The fairly sparse decoration is vaguely Jacobean but the complex structure of three semicircular towers and two intermediate flat towers adds interest to a wide case.

Back in 1877 the architect Sir Thomas Jackson had also used Renaissance elements in his design for the organ in Wren's Sheldonian Theatre, Oxford. He produced a more overtly Jacobean design for his 1886 case to the organ in Wadham College Chapel but moved into the next century for his 1892 double-fronted case in Brasenose College Chapel. The east face, in particular, with its short wide towers, is very reminiscent of the eighteenth-century south German organs of Gottfried Silbermann. However, unlike Silbermann's organs, the front pipes are all so short that the lowest notes had to be elsewhere.

Hull City Hall: Philip H. Selfe, 1911.
Organ by Forster & Andrews. (Drawing by Philip H. Selfe)

Brasenose College Chapel, Oxford:
Thomas Jackson, 1892.
Organ by Hill & Son.

The inspiration for Brasenose Chapel? Grosshartmannsdorf, Saxony, Germany: Gottfried Silbermann, 1741.
(Photo: Peter Williams)

76   The Box of Whistles

*Hampstead Parish Church, London:
Thomas Jackson, c.1884. Organ by Henry Willis.*

Jackson turned to English seventeenth-century practice for his case at Hampstead Parish Church. With its central round tower, flanked by double-storey flats and V-shape outer towers, it is remarkable chiefly for the pavilions over the towers as well as exuberant carving which extends even to the upright members of the case.

For his large 16 ft case for the organ in Bath Abbey in 1914, Jackson moderated his style to suit the organ's environment, introducing Gothic carving as vestigial doors to soften the tower sides, but using very un-Gothic arches over the flats. The chair case was added in 1972, designed by Alan Rome after a sketch by Herbert Norman. The drawing shows the main case with the original zinc front pipes with the mouth line in the towers and upper flats running the wrong way. This was corrected in 1997 when they were replaced by new tin-metal pipes with the longest pipes having the shortest feet, giving the case a cheerful face instead of a glum one.

The 1920s were a relatively fallow period. One of the most extraordinary examples of an organ used as an excuse to construct an over-scaled decoration was the work of the architects Lanchester, Lucas & Lodge at the Third Church of Christ Scientist, Curzon Street, London. In

*Bath Abbey: main case by Thomas Jackson, 1914.
Chair case by Alan Rome/Herbert Norman, 1972.
(Drawing by Herbert Norman)*

Not all Gothic 77

1933 the architect of the large chapel of the Royal Naval School, Holbrook, near Ipswich, could only repeat Scott's essay at Camberwell 89 years before and provide a huge timber grille for the equally large four-manual organ, not a single pipe being visible.

Meanwhile, Philip Selfe, by then at Hill Norman & Beard, designed a number of modest vaguely Gothic cases, one of the most successful being at St James, Riddlesdown, Surrey. W. D. Caroe was, however, still active and, also in 1933, produced an original double-sided case for the organ on the screen of Southwell Minster, Nottinghamshire. The organ stands on the screen, at the junction of the Romanesque

Third Church of Christ Scientist, Curzon Street, London: Lanchester, Lucas & Lodge, 1928. Organ by Norman & Beard, 1911. Organ no longer extant. (Photo: Hill Norman & Beard)

St James, Riddlesdown, Surrey: Philip H. Selfe, 1932. Organ by Hill Norman & Beard. (Photo: Hill Norman & Beard)

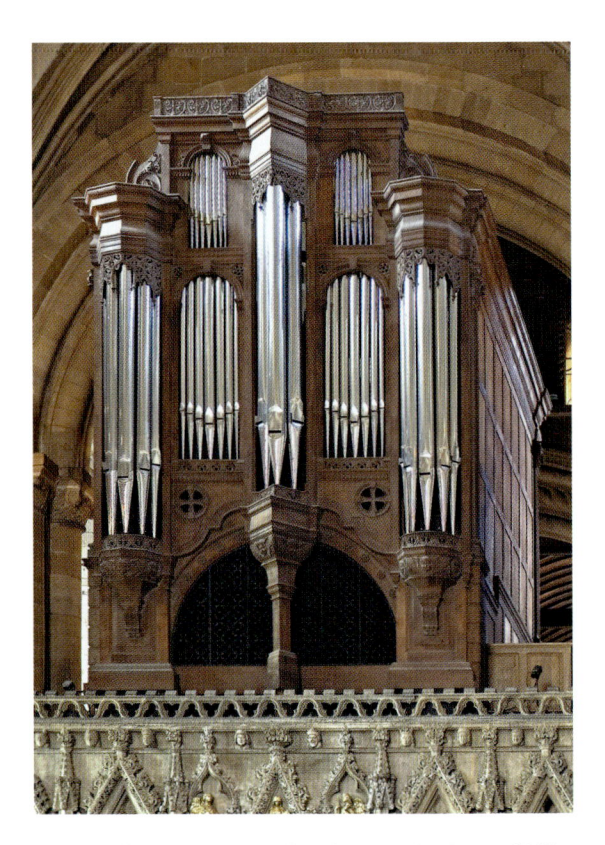

Southwell Minster, Nottinghamshire: W. D. Caroe, 1933. Organ by Hill Norman & Beard. Tin-alloy front pipes by Nicholson, 1996. (Photo: Chris Knapton)

St John the Baptist, Lound: Sir Ninian Comper, 1913. Organ by Harrison & Harrison. (Photo: Andrew Hayden)

nave and the Gothic Quire and the case combines Renaissance and Gothic elements in an original way. The semicircular opening in the lower part of the case is a Caroe peculiarity. As originally built it bore little relationship to the layout of the instrument inside, though this has now changed to take advantage of the opening. The front pipes were originally all dull zinc, but the west-facing pipes (all dummy) were covered in polished tin sheet in 1971 and the east-facing fronts replaced by tin-metal pipes in 1996.

Another architect who attempted a synthesis of Gothic and Renaissance styles was Sir Ninian Comper. Often complex in design, his organ cases were pure screens, beautifully decorated but bearing little relationship to the instruments behind them. The front pipes were frequently no more than half the size of real pipes in order to compress the design into the space available. As explained in Chapter 2, this seriously distorts the width-to-length proportions of the pipes. Although the organ at Lound, Suffolk, photographs well, because one has no yardstick by which to judge the scale, the result is inevitably false when seen in the building.

The high point of the pre-war period was the double-fronted main case and east-side chair case of the organ on the screen in Norwich Cathedral, designed by Stephen Dykes-Bower in 1939–40 but not completed until 1950. Dykes-Bower took the bold decision, in a Romanesque building, to build in a seventeenth-century style. As has been noted before, this style has sufficient Gothic structures within it to succeed in such an environment. The east face and the chair case have a definite Harris feel about them, with elements of Gloucester in the central tower and Emmanuel College, Cambridge, in the chair. The west face is more Smith-like although the pointed compartments between the towers are original. The Restoration custom of placing a crown on the central tower is repeated on the west face; this had to be placed in position in the dead of night while an anti-monarchist member of the Chapter was absent! The gilded star was added in 1970. It rotates when a stop which sounds small bells is drawn. Dykes-Bower suggested the spikes which project between the points of the star.

However, just as in the second half of the nineteenth century, many organs for ordinary churches continued to be made without proper cases. Indeed the only difference in the twentieth century was that the appearance was still plainer because it became usual to follow the practice, described in Chapter 6, of supporting the front pipes from behind with no visible stay in front of them. The 1902 Norman

Norwich Cathedral (east face):
Stephen Dykes-Bower, 1940–50.
Organ by Hill Norman & Beard.
(By permission of the Dean and Chapter)

Norwich Cathedral, detail of west face
showing crown: cymbelstern star added in
1970. (By permission of the Dean and Chapter)

& Beard instrument in All Saints, Notting Hill, London, may be taken as typical. The absence of upper casework on a single-storey front leads to considerable false over-length in order to create enough height to cover the internal pipes. Later cases had even more pipes of apparently the same length, leading to problems of pipe-speech in pipes whose speaking length was a fraction of their physical length.

This sort of organ front has proved particularly unfortunate if the instrument is placed in front of a window. The light from behind, shining through between the front pipes, gives them the appearance of a paling fence. Another feature that makes these instruments look boring is that front pipe decoration went out of fashion about 1900 and, as noted in Chapter 7, plain unpainted zinc soon oxidized to a dull matt grey surface.

Sometimes the 'pipe-rack' effect arose by accident, when a planned organ case was completed only as far as the impost, leaving gaps

Occasional attempts were made to hide parts of organs behind pre-existing stonework. The bass pipes peeping through a medieval window in St Mary Redcliffe, Bristol, are perhaps an extreme example.

With the rise of modernist architecture, some people at first saw plain pipe-racks as the way forward. A case in point is the main organ at Guildford Cathedral (1961), though here, as in many places, the bare zinc was relieved by spraying the pipes with metallic paint.

A more imaginative development of this approach was used in the then new Coventry Cathedral in 1962. Here the bass pipes stand in interleaved groups, giving their appearance considerably more variety than would otherwise be possible without casework. This style does have the problem, however, that it is essentially a two-dimensional approach to a three-dimensional object; as soon as one moves to the side, the support structures start to become evident (see overleaf).

All Saints, Notting Hill, London: attributed to C. Hodgson Fowler. Organ by Norman & Beard, 1902.

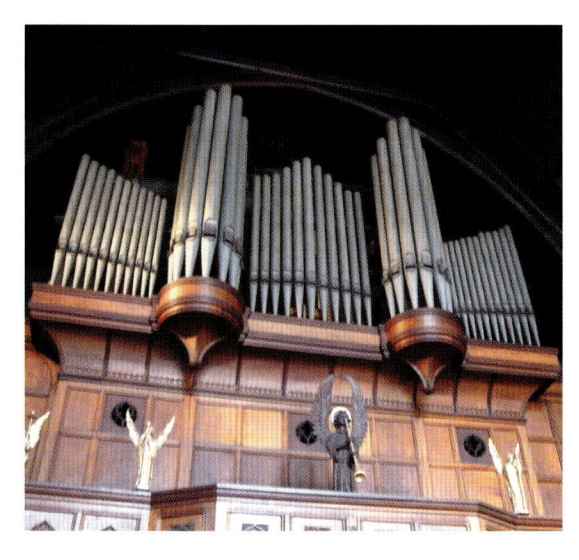

Christ Church, Isle of Dogs, London: designer unknown, c.1900. Organ rebuilt by T. C. Lewis.

where the uprights that were to support upper casework never arrived. This can be seen, for instance, in the instrument at Christ Church, Isle of Dogs, London.

St Mary Redcliffe, Bristol: Harrison & Harrison, 1912.

Not all Gothic   81

*Coventry Cathedral:
Basil Spence/Cuthbert Harrison, 1962.
Organ by Harrison & Harrison.*

Ultimately, the boring appearance of organs without upper casework and the falsities involved in over-length pipes sounded the death-knell of this style and, as we will see in the next two chapters, artists searched for new inspiration for the appearance of the organ.

9
AMERICAN SHOWMANSHIP REVEALS ALL

The reaction to the dull fences of pipes described in the previous chapter, many of them dummies, came first from America, where Walter Holtkamp (1894–1962) gave the opinion: 'I don't want my tone mixed, pre-digested and rendered into an impersonal mass. I prefer to sit in the same room with the pipes and do my own mixing.'

The normal layout of an organ has many of the largest pipes at the front and smaller ones at the back. Holtkamp developed a style of organ layout in which every pipe was seen, the small treble pipes right at the front with the bass pipes to the back. The layout of the soundboard was varied, using electric action, to produce the best massing of large numbers of small pipes.

Actually, this was not entirely a new idea. George Jardine built an organ for St George's Episcopal Church, New York, in 1869, very much in this style and, in London, Proms concertgoers will have noted that there are many interior pipes visible in the centre of Father Willis's 1871 organ in the Royal Albert Hall.

Walter Holtkamp built his first organ on this principle back in 1928 and the idea was copied first in Holland and then, in 1932, by Klais in

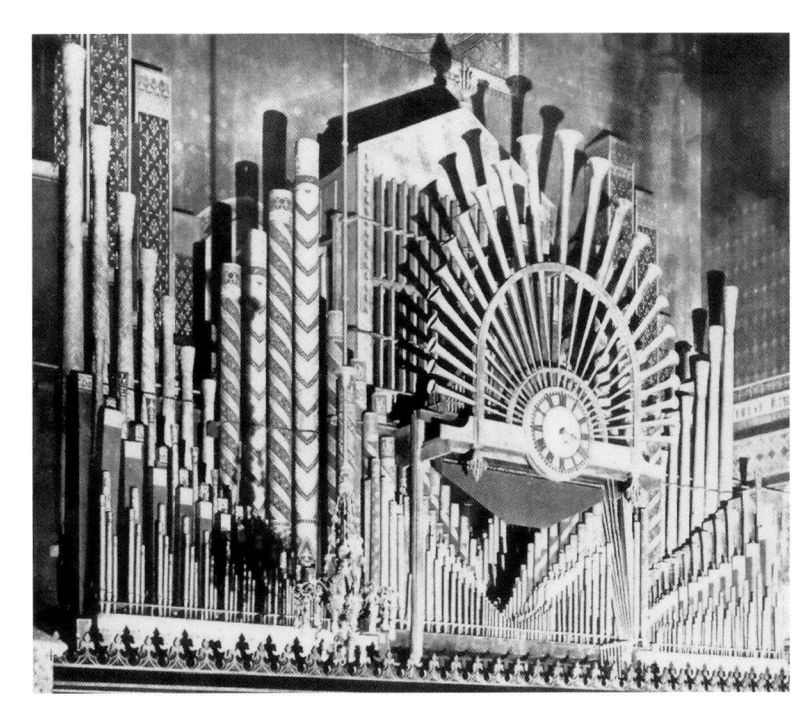

St George's Episcopal Church, New York: George Jardine, 1869. Organ no longer extant.

Germany. Holtkamp's 1955 organ in the chapel of the Massachusetts Institute of Technology, Cambridge, Massachusetts achieved wide publicity and showed how well this style could combine with minimalist architecture.

Although Holtkamp built no organs for Britain, he influenced many other builders and a number of instruments based on his ideas were built here in the period 1950–1970. The Rushworth & Dreaper 1961 detached Choir organ in Guildford Cathedral is a notable example, with a particularly simple outline, standing on a tribune on the north side of the chancel. Peter Wood used a similar design for the Choir organ at Frant Parish Church in East Sussex.

A larger instrument in this style, also from 1961, is the Hill Norman & Beard organ in the Mormon Hyde Park Chapel, Kensington, London, designed by Herbert Norman. Here the instrument is spread across the front of a wide but low building. The appearance is not quite as honest as it seems, as one dummy bass pipe was needed to complete the design.

Frant Parish Church, East Sussex (Choir organ): Peter Wood, 1968.

Hyde Park Chapel (Mormon), Exhibition Road, Kensington: Herbert Norman, 1961. Organ by Hill Norman & Beard.

84 The Box of Whistles

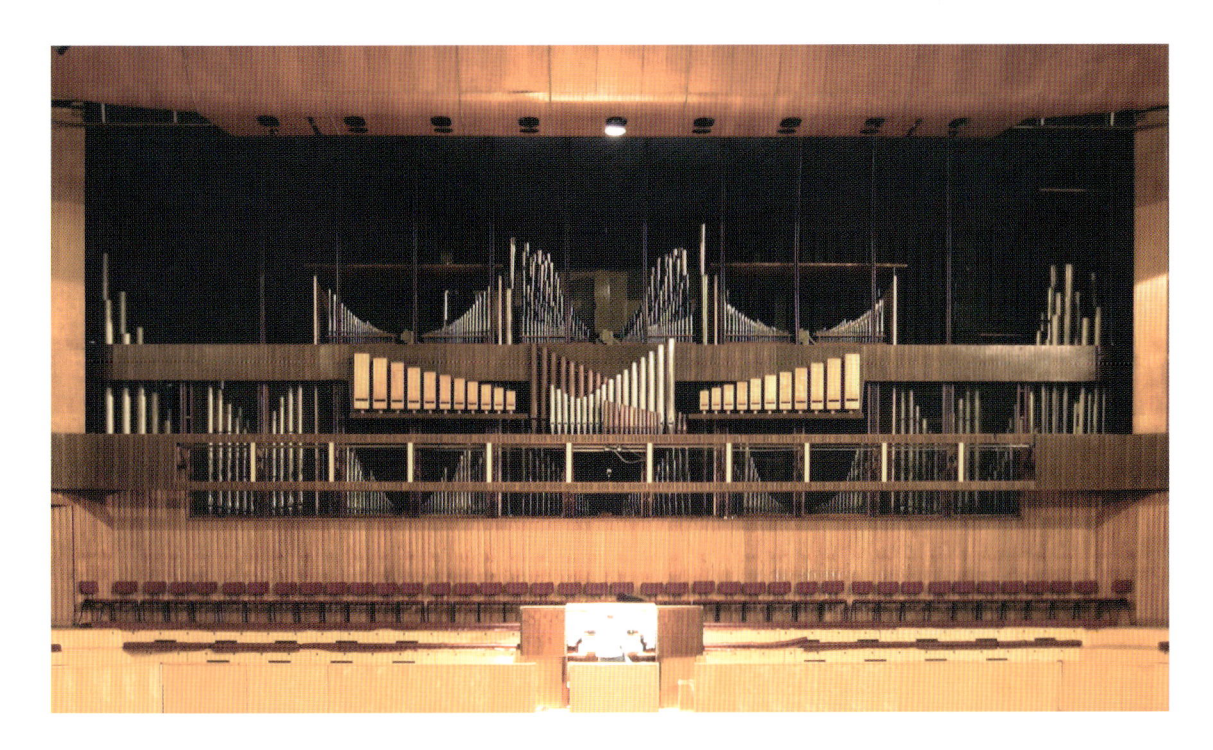

Royal Festival Hall, London: Sir Leslie Martin / Cuthbert Harrison, 1954. Organ by Harrison & Harrison. (Photos: William McVicker)

The organ that most people associate with this exposed style is the Harrison & Harrison instrument in the Royal Festival Hall, London, completed in 1954. This was, however, not the intention of its designers. Initial sketches with just a dull screen of bass pipes never quite satisfied all parties. With the opening date looming, Cuthbert Harrison despaired of agreement and laid out the organ to be hidden behind an anonymous grille. At the very last moment, the then Leader of the London County Council demanded to be able to see his 'expensive pipes', so the grille was omitted and the open display came about, virtually by accident. The 'motif' of very obviously dummy pipes, hiding the bellows, was designed by Sir Leslie Martin. The appearance of this instrument is now undergoing further change consequent on alterations to the hall to increase space for orchestral players.

What is sometimes called the neo-Holtkamp style can look attractive when arranged spaciously in a modernist building. However, the appearance looks less happy when the pipes have dulled with time and, although still sometimes employed in America, it fell out of favour here after 1970.

American showmanship

10
THE NEW BRUTALISM (AND AFTER)

Two trends came together to guide the formation of the case style that dominated the 1960s and 1970s. First, a growing interest in the music of Bach's time led organbuilding in a new direction, paralleling an increasing interest in early music. The effect on organ design was profound. The instrument again became a free-standing piece of furniture with a vertical rather than a horizontal layout. Where possible, one division does not stand in front of another so the organ is very shallow and the tone not diffused. Following the *Werkprinzip* described at the end of Chapter 1, each division normally occupies a separate case or obvious division of the main case, each with its own roof. The so-called 'tone cabinet' has important acoustic effects adding warmth and resonance, the latter being especially noticeable in a dry acoustic. This is because all the sound energy is thrown forward so that less is wasted in the rafters; the pipes need be blown less hard, giving a warmer sound. The sound is also aided by the low-frequency air resonances characteristic of enclosed spaces.

The *Werkprinzip* discipline strongly dictated the case outline, often giving the instrument a distinctive three-dimensional silhouette. Although only a minority of the instruments were for new buildings, many case designers followed a modernist trend and relied on the silhouette to provide the main visual interest of the instrument, keeping timber sections and mouldings as simple as possible. Decoration was often confined to pipe-shades, occasionally using copper or other metals as an alternative to pierced wood.

The first cases of this type originated in Scandinavia. The one-manual 1959 organ in the Danish Seamen's Church in London came from the Copenhagen firm of Frobenius. It has a strong, simple, asymmetric yet waisted

Danish Seamen's Church, London: Erik Frobenius, 1959. Organ by Frobenius, Copenhagen. (Drawing by John Brennan)

St George, Dunster, Somerset: Herbert Norman, 1960. (Drawing by Herbert Norman)

*St Peter, Vere Street, London: John Muir, 1965.
Organ rebuilt by Hill Norman & Beard. The instrument is
now in Lancashire. (Photo: Hill Norman & Beard)*

silhouette with the front pipes in six groups. This gives large differences in both length and diameter between adjacent pipes.

The Church of St George, Dunster, Somerset, has one of the first modernist cases by a British builder. This quite simple case by Herbert Norman, dated 1960, is given distinction by the Spanish-type horizontal trumpet pipes projecting from it. These pipes are supported by a hidden frame held up by steel piano wire.

Another modernist case with horizontal trumpets was that designed by the architect John Muir for St Peter's Church, Vere Street, London. There was no attempt here at the *Werkprinzip*, just a bold and simple outline with the front edge of the centre compartment covered in the same aluminium leaf that was used as the front pipe finish.

The organ in the chapel of Clare College, Cambridge (1968) was designed by Rudolph von Beckerath of Hamburg, the Hanseatic home of the *Werkprinzip*. There was space here to express the style in all its clarity, the large towers to each side containing the Pedal organ, the upper case the Great organ, with the Swell department

*Clare College Chapel, Cambridge: R. von Beckerath, 1968.
Organ by Beckerath, Hamburg.*

*St Martin le Grand, York: George Pace/staff of
J. W. Walker, 1968. (Photo: J. W. Walker & Sons)*

The new brutalism 87

New College Chapel, Oxford: George Pace and Frank Bradbeer, 1969. Organ by Grant, Degens & Bradbeer.

beneath revealing exposed shutter louvres. But, in such a building, did it really have to be so brutal?

George Pace worked with the staff of J. W. Walker & Sons to produce a really original and visually acceptable instrument for the medieval church of St Martin le Grand, York, in 1968. The use of glass and metal in this strikingly simple (if slightly neo-Holtkamp) case would not be out of place in a post-modern building of the twenty-first century. But how would it translate to a bigger instrument?

The use of metal instead of wood is also a feature of the 1969 instrument in the chapel of New College, Oxford. In such august surroundings, it took real courage to choose a modernist case. This did not, however, deter George Pace, who designed the organ case in conjunction with Frank Bradbeer. The Pedal towers are at the side, the Great organ on top and the projecting chair case houses the *Rückpositiv* division. The enclosed Swell organ integrates well but reflections off the exposed glass louvre shutters cause the north windows of the chapel to appear to chase one another across the front of the organ whenever the shutters are moved by the player. The rear aspect, from the antechapel, illustrates the problems of incorporating a modernist case into a Gothic environment.

Left to himself, Frank Bradbeer always designed cases that are models of simplicity. This is particularly evident in his case for the organ in the Lyons Concert Hall, University of York. Here, with both height and width available, the organ is very shallow, being laid out on a wall not a floor, with the separate sections of the organ clearly visible in its appearance. The three manual departments are in the centre, one above another, and the Pedal organ, with its large bass pipes, is arranged in the side panels.

Not only do some organbuilders feel that the air resonances in tightly fitting tone cabinets enhance the warmth of sound but, in addition, one of the advantages of the modernist style is that it is relatively easy to accommodate an asymmetric layout. The construction and disposition of the tone cabinets are clearly exposed in the 1970 organ in Carrs Lane

Lyons Concert Hall, University of York: Frank Bradbeer, 1969. Organ by Grant, Degens & Bradbeer. (Photo: © University of York)

Carrs Lane Church, Birmingham: John Norman, 1970. Organ by Hill Norman & Beard.

The new brutalism 89

Anglican Chapel, HMS Neptune naval base, Faslane, Scotland: Kenneth Prior, 1969. Organ by Hill Norman & Beard.

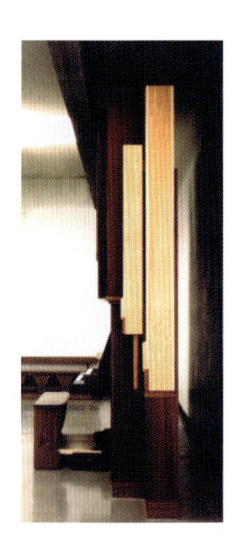

Church, Birmingham. Building on an asymmetric arrangement of the internal pipes, tightly fitting tone cabinets (one for each manual and one for the Pedal organ) combine to form a solid sculpture. In this instrument an electric action was used to minimize the space occupied by the mechanism.

Another organ that exploited an extremely compact mechanism is the instrument in the Anglican Chapel at HMS Neptune, the naval base in Faslane, Scotland. The pipes of the Great organ are divided either side of the box containing the Swell organ (with exposed louvres), with the wooden bass pedal pipes at the ends. In this way Kenneth Prior achieved an exceptionally shallow layout, as shown in the right-hand photograph.

The 1972 organ in the then new St Mark's Church, North End, Portsmouth, is much less brutal than the Carrs Lane organ but similarly asymmetric, compactly arranged on a shelf at the side of the sanctuary. Herbert Norman accommodated this layout by using modernist freedom to create an asymmetric case. The case is of Douglas fir and the front pipes of tin metal, spotted metal and copper. The design of the hexagonal towers is loosely based on the transept

St Mark, North End, Portsmouth: Herbert Norman, 1972. Organ by Hill Norman & Beard. (Drawing by Herbert Norman)

Robinson College Chapel, Cambridge: Erik Frobenius, 1981. Organ by Frobenius, Copenhagen.

Clifton Cathedral, Bristol: J. von Glatter-Götz, 1973. Organ by Rieger, Schwarzach, Austria.

Church of the Resurrection, Bayside, Dublin: Andrew Pennells, 1996. Organ by J. W. Walker. (Photo: J. W. Walker & Sons)

organ in Freiburg Minster. Pipe-shades are reintroduced but placed behind the front pipes, leaving their natural length exposed.

The Roman Catholic Cathedral in Clifton, Bristol, completed in 1973, has a remarkable asymmetric organ case by Joseph von Glatter-Götz of Rieger Orgelbau in Austria. The Pedal tower, with its staggered row of copper front pipes, is rather heavy and overbearing but the three angled towers, constructed very simply

The new brutalism 91

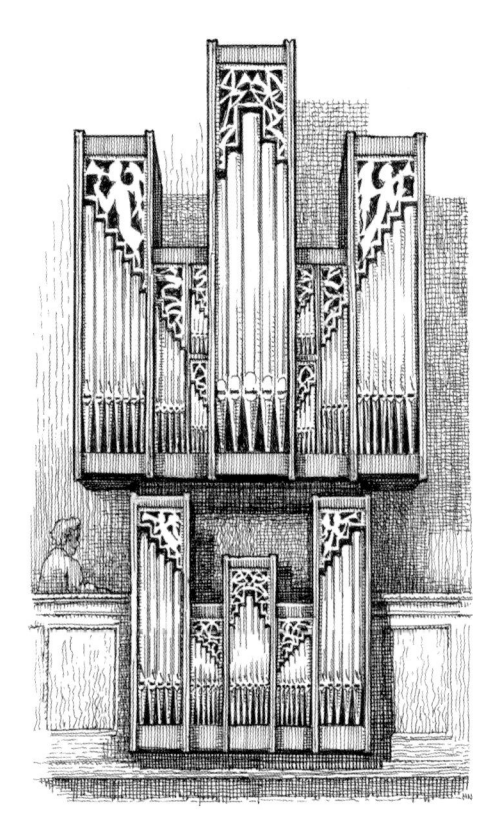

Church of the Sacred Heart, Henley-on-Thames: Peter Collins, 1976. Organ by Peter Collins. (Drawing by Herbert Norman)

St Stephen, Derby: Roger Pulham, 1983. Organ by Roger Pulham. (Photo: Roger Pulham)

of veneered blockboard, have a theatricality which matches this innovative building very well.

Yet another asymmetric case arrived rather later, in 1981, in Robinson College, Cambridge. It maintains a Scandinavian simplicity (one might almost call it severity) characteristic of its origins. The case was designed by Erik Frobenius of Copenhagen in conjunction with Gillespie Kidd & Coia, architects of the chapel.

A late example of the Scandinavian-style case is that designed for the 1970s Church of the Resurrection, Bayside, Dublin, by Andrew Pennells of J. W. Walker in 1996. The style was deliberately adopted to blend with the 25-year-old building. The organ stands in front of a recess, so is less shallow than appears. In order to obtain the right relationship between the case size and the building, the longest pipe in the case is bottom E, the lowest four pipes being inside.

The tendency in the later 1970s was, however, to move away from brutalism and reintroduce some discipline and a modest degree of decoration. The west gallery of the Church of the Sacred Heart, Henley-on-Thames, has a Peter Collins organ of 1976 with a pair of cases combining a classic double-organ layout with modernist simplicity. The fretted pipe-shades are particularly successful, relieving the simplicity of the basic structure.

The pipe-shades of the organ in the Church of St Stephen, Derby, are also based on flying

Turner Sims Concert Hall, University of Southampton: Peter Collins, 1977. Organ by Peter Collins.
(Photo: Peter Collins)

Church of the Holy Cross, Fenham, Newcastle upon Tyne: Roger Pulham, 1981. Organ by Church & Co.
(Photo: Nigel Church/Lammermuir Pipe Organs)

angels, carved in bas-relief without any added decoration. This case was designed by Roger Pulham who has combined careers in both architecture and organbuilding.

The Peter Collins organ in the Turner Sims Concert Hall, University of Southampton, was built the year after Henley. It combines simplicity of outline (like Bradbeer's case at York) with a relatively sophisticated layout of front pipes and pipe-shades. This instrument has one division placed below the impost, a relatively short-lived fashion which faded after about 1980.

The combination of a strong outline with a more sophisticated shape produced the instrument in the Church of the Holy Cross, Fenham, Newcastle upon Tyne, designed by Roger Pulham for Nigel Church. The wing-like side compartments are balanced by a small central tower. The pipe-shades are placed behind

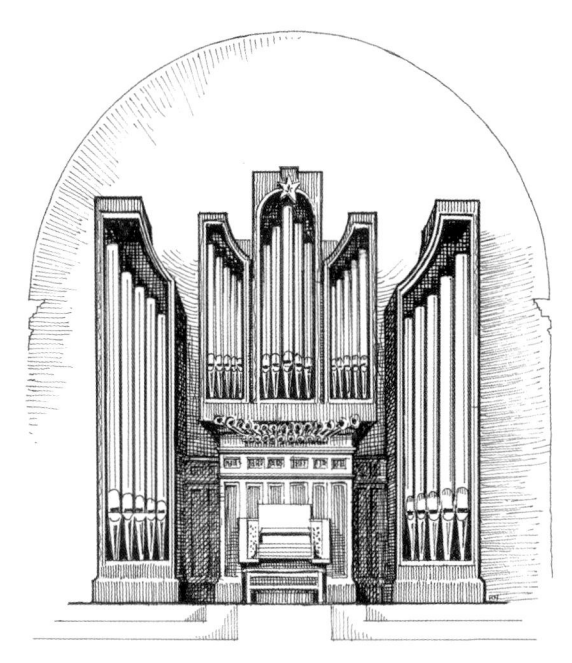

Pritchard-Jones Hall, University of Bangor, North Wales: Herbert Norman, 1973. Organ by Hill Norman & Beard.
(Drawing by Herbert Norman)

The new brutalism 93

St Peter Mancroft, Norwich: Peter Collins, 1984.
Organ by Peter Collins.

City of London School: David Graebe, 1987.
Organ by J. W. Walker.

the front pipes, filling the space over the pipe-tops but not concealing the mild asymmetry arising from equivalent pipes on each side actually speaking notes a semitone apart.

Herbert Norman achieved a similar winged effect in his case for the organ in the Pritchard-Jones Hall, Bangor University, North Wales. This combines a more prominent central tower with separate side towers for the 16 ft bass pipes of the Pedal organ. The design includes both horizontal trumpets and a cymbelstern.

The visual separation of departments was taken a stage further in the Peter Collins organ at the west end of the Perpendicular church of St Peter Mancroft in the centre of Norwich. This has the classic *Werkprinzip* layout with four separate cases, the player being concealed by the small chair case. To fit closely against the tower arch, the large Pedal organ towers on each side were made diagonal, involving an original layout for the mechanism. Here the pipe-shades are neither in front nor behind the front pipes but hover above them. The pipe-shades for the main cases were designed by Herbert Norman and those on the chair case by the carver, Siegfried Pietszch.

David Graebe has been a most prolific designer over the past 25 years. The 1987 Walker organ in the Great Hall of the new City of London School has a complex and interesting case by him. The *Werkprinzip* layout is very evident in this case also, with the three manual divisions arranged vertically and cantilevered Pedal organ towers at the sides. As with many

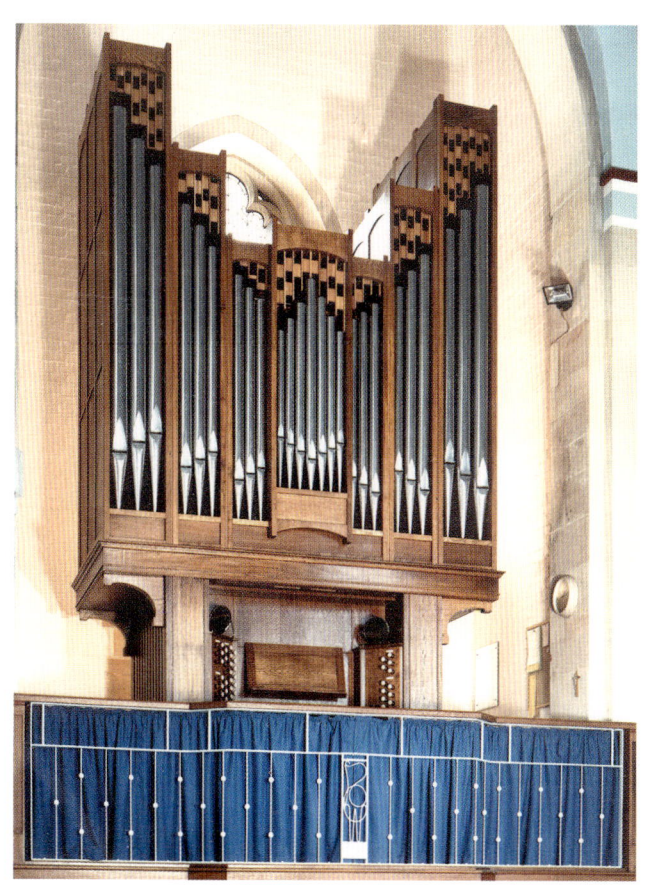

*St Mildred, Addiscombe, Surrey: Stephen Bicknell, 1988.
Organ by N. P. Mander. (Photo: Mander Organs)*

*St James, South Anston, Yorkshire:
Ronald Sims, 1990. Organ by
Roger Pulham. (Photo: Roger Pulham)*

modernist cases at this time, the posts go past the horizontal members at the cornices, providing a hint of pinnacles. The horizontal trumpets should be noted, a recurring theme.

The case of the east-end organ at St Mildred's Church, Addiscombe, Surrey was designed by Stephen Bicknell and the organ built by Mander in 1988. This is another instrument combining a classic organ outline, going back to medieval Gothic, but with a blurred distinction between towers and flats and with modernist detail, this time in a 1930s simplified Gothic church. The curved heads to the side panels echo domestic window detail current in the 1980s.

The organ on the west gallery of St James's Church, South Anston, Yorkshire has a much less conservative outline even though it is based on the centuries old double organ layout with a chair case in front. Built by Roger Pulham in 1990, both case and gallery were designed by Ronald Sims. The organ reflects an increasing trend towards a degree of ornamentation, even on a modernist case. The emphasis on the diagonals created by the lines of the pipe-tops is unusual and is reminiscent of the New College, Oxford, case designed by Sims's former partner, George Pace.

Although the instrument inside it was not completed until 2001, the case of the organ in Symphony Hall, Birmingham, by Klais of Bonn, Germany, dates from 1991. Much larger in scale than most church organs, the longest internal pipes having bodies 32 ft (nearly 10 m) in length, it was clearly designed to fit closely with the architecture of the hall. Unusually for a modern case it is not entirely free-standing. The device

The new brutalism

Symphony Hall, Birmingham:
Ralph Schweitzer and Philipp Klais, 1991.
Organ by Orgelbau Klais, Bonn, completed 2001.
(Photo: Mike Gutteridge/Orgelbau Klais)

Petersfield Parish Church, Hampshire:
Neil Richerby, 1992. Pipe-shades by John
Brennan, organ by Lammermuir Pipe Organs.
(Photo: Mark Dancer)

of using dummy extensions of the pipes as pipe-shades is one that Klais has used elsewhere.

Neil Richerby designed the case of the 1992 Lammermuir organ in Petersfield Parish Church, Hampshire. The two larger 'boxes' on the left front the Pedal organ and the three on the right contain the Great organ. The Swell division is hidden behind. The simple modern design of the pipe-shades is effective and the pipes are placed in front of them so that the natural lengths of the pipes are visible.

By contrast, the case of the organ on the west gallery of the new Church of St Paul, Harringay, London, is of extreme simplicity, matching the design of the west end of the church where it is placed. Designed by Richard Bower in conjunction with Peter Jenkins, architect of the church, and completed in 1993, it eschews pipe-shades. Although this reveals the front of the Swell organ, placed in the top of the instrument, the swellbox shutters are painted black, as are the wooden Pedal pipes on show in the two side wings. Competition from the light of the windows at the side of the instrument renders them almost invisible.

*St Paul, Harringay, London:
Richard Bower/Peter Jenkins, 1993. Organ by Bower & Co.*

Also painted black, the striking case of the 1995 Nicholson organ in St Bartholomew, Westhoughton, Lancashire, was designed by Anthony Hall. A classic layout of towers and two-storey flats is combined with modernist detail to match its surroundings. The way height is gained by exaggerating the length of the pipe-shades is quite original.

Kenneth Tickell has a way of designing cases that combine classical principles with modernist detail. Nowhere is this more evident than in his 1994 organ which stands adjacent to the contemporary extension to Douai Abbey, Berkshire. This much-admired instrument has a two-storey central tower, reflecting the interior layout on three levels, the lowest of which speaks out through the carved grille above the console. The modernist pipe-shades and grille-work are particularly notable and were designed by Alan Caiger-Smith.

Another instrument by the same designer, also with a case based on classical principles, can be found in the new Church of St Barnabas, Dulwich. Completed in 1997, this instrument has a

*St Bartholomew, Westhoughton, Lancashire:
Anthony Hall, 1995. Organ by Nicholson.
(Photo: Ross Young/Nicholson & Co.)*

substantial case with 16 ft pipes on display. Tickell used flamed copper for the Pedal pipes, so that the Great and Choir departments stand out by the use of burnished tin metal. The front pipes are natural length, so there is a subtle difference between the otherwise symmetrical towers.

We have largely confined ourselves to Britain in this survey but a very distinctive-looking organ was made in London by Mander in 1997 for the west gallery of Urakami Cathedral, Japan. The case, designed by Didier Grassin with a bold modern approach to detail, contrasts pipe-caps of oak-faced plywood (with a hint of origami) with burnished tin front pipes. The use of a chair case for part of the instrument has helped to make the most of the restricted height.

Douai Abbey, Berkshire: Kenneth Tickell, 1994.
Organ by Kenneth Tickell & Co.
(Photo: Kenneth Tickell)

Douai Abbey: pipe-shade detail by
Alan Caiger-Smith.
(Photo: Kenneth Tickell)

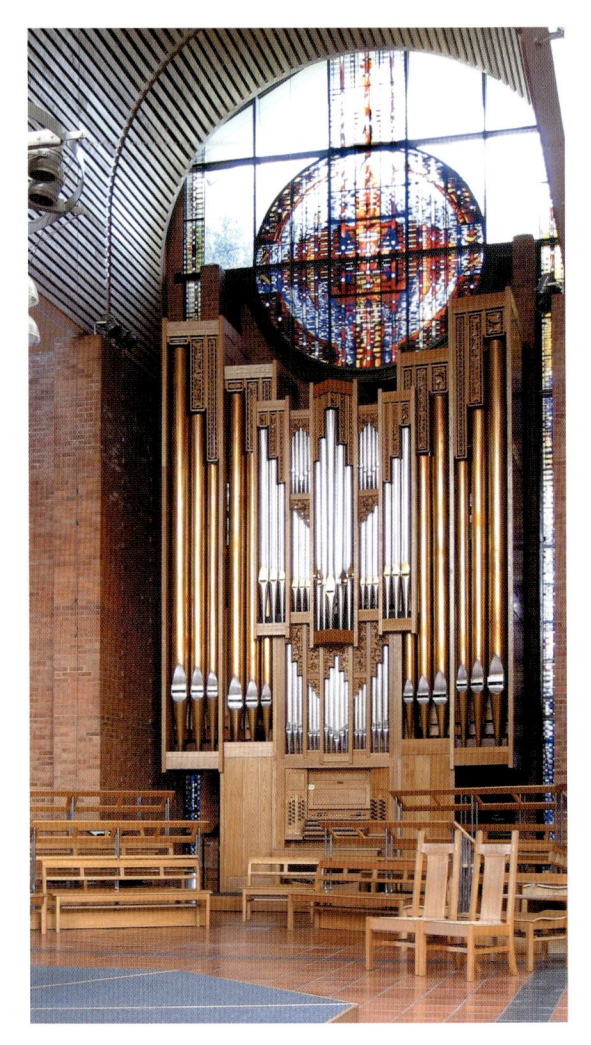

St Barnabas, Dulwich:
Kenneth Tickell, 1997.
Organ by Kenneth Tickell & Co.
(Photo: Kenneth Tickell)

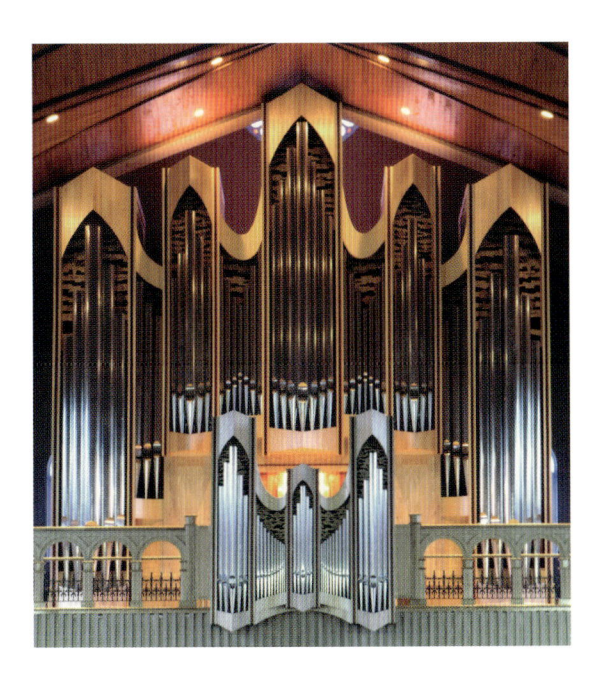

*Urakami Cathedral, Japan: Didier Grassin, 1997.
Organ by N. P. Mander. (Photo: Mander Organs)*

*Worcester Cathedral, nave organ.
Draft design by Didier Grassin, 2003,
for Nicholson & Co.*

*St Mary, Hendon: Nicholas Plumley, 1999.
Organ by Peter Collins. (Photo: Peter Collins)*

The 1999 Peter Collins organ in St Mary's Church, Hendon, Middlesex, has a case designed by Nicholas Plumley. It is remarkably free-form and stands with its departments at varying angles to the prevailing axes of the building. It required considerable bravery to commission a case of this type for a medieval church, even if the organ actually stands in an Edwardian addition. The flowing coloured pipe-shades provide a unifying factor to otherwise slightly jumbled elevations.

Over the years, the modernist style has clearly evolved from its simple but relatively brutal beginnings, yet the number of its exponents now seems to be on the decline. Didier Grassin's design for the new nave organ at Worcester Cathedral has attracted both enthusiastic support and negative opposition. By contrast to these problems, in the next chapter we consider the ways in which case designs based on historical models have evolved over the last 40 years.

The new brutalism

11
PRESENT-DAY ECLECTICISM

At the same time as the modernist movement was having its effect on organ design, some designers continued to create organ cases using traditional design forms. This has been especially common where the location is an existing non-modernist building. Nevertheless, nothing artistic is ever static for long and mere copying is but a sterile art. An increasing eclecticism has combined elements from various historic sources to create quite original designs which, in many cases, are still capable of complementing historic buildings.

Stephen Dykes-Bower's earlier work was described in Chapter 8. One of his last major commissions was the highly architectural case for the organ in the hall of the Worshipful Company of Merchant Taylors, in the City of London. It combines an Italianate pediment, uprights in the form of classical pilasters and early eighteenth-century oval panels of pipes with pipe-shades in the form of imitation drapery. The lavish use of colour is a trademark of Dykes-Bower's work.

The other thing that is different about the Merchant Taylors' Hall case is that, unlike some other Dykes-Bower examples, such as in Great Yarmouth Parish Church, the case is not just a mere screen but is an integral part of a free-standing instrument. With its great overhangs, the case is so free-standing, in fact, that it looks rather as if it might fall over! This move back to free-standing cases resulted from the influence of the Continental *Werkprinzip*, as described in the last chapter. It is perhaps appropriate that this point is made particularly clear by the case of the Danish-made organ that was completed in 1965 in Queen's College Chapel, Oxford. This instrument looks, at first sight, as if it is three organs. The central part is the main organ; the upper case, with its three main and two vestigial towers, contains the pipes of the Great organ (lower manual). The vertically extended lower case contains the pipes of the 'Brustpositive' (upper manual) in a louvred swellbox behind the fretted opening. The two side cases contain the pipes of the Pedal organ, with alternate notes either side.

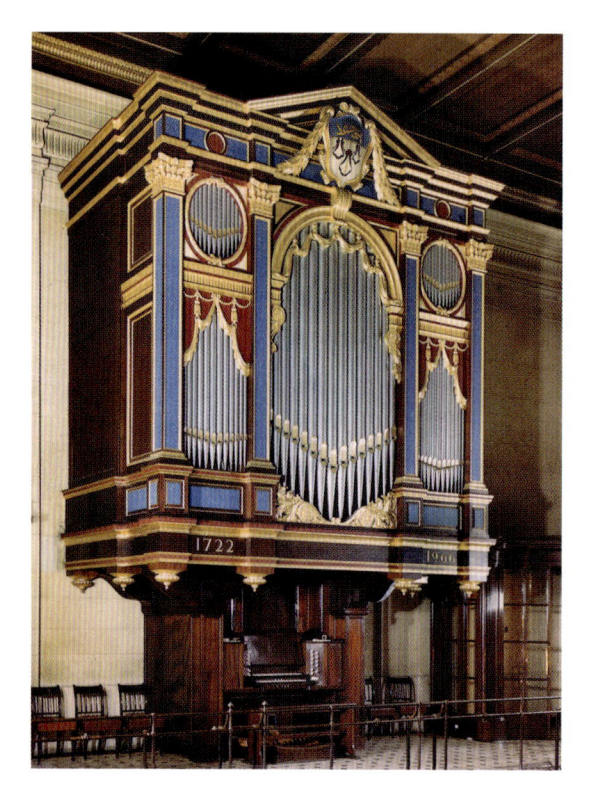

Merchant Taylors' Hall, City of London:
Stephen Dykes-Bower, 1966. Organ by N. P. Mander.
(Photo: Mander Organs)

100 The Box of Whistles

Queen's College Chapel, Oxford: Fin Ditlevsen, 1965. Organ by Frobenius, Copenhagen.

Merton College Chapel, Oxford: Robert Potter, 1968. Organ by J. W. Walker. (Photo: J. W. Walker & Sons)

Sadly, other work by Continental organbuilders in a traditional style has not always been entirely happy, sometimes as a result of the enlargement of a historic case to permit a larger instrument. An example of this, also in Oxford, was the 1979 reconstruction of the organ in Christ Church Cathedral that involved the jacking up of the 1680s Father Smith main case to permit the insertion of an out-of-scale series of carved panels below the impost. This additionally had the result of destroying the vertical relationship between the main and chair cases. A similar problem arose at St John's, Smith Square, London in 1993, where the main case (Jordan, Byfield and Bridge, 1733) was elevated to gallery parapet level. At St Marylebone Parish Church, London, the 1987 organ was all new but its size nevertheless presented problems and the three-compartment-wide two-storey central tower is so imposing that it almost appears to be supporting the church ceiling.

Returning to Oxford, Robert Potter used a somewhat etiolated Gothic for his case for the organ in Merton College Chapel in 1968. The design feels more like 1830, although quite unlike any cases that were actually being made

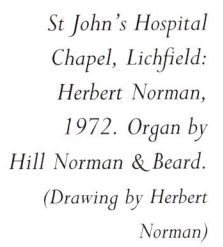

St John's Hospital Chapel, Lichfield: Herbert Norman, 1972. Organ by Hill Norman & Beard. (Drawing by Herbert Norman)

Present-day eclecticism 101

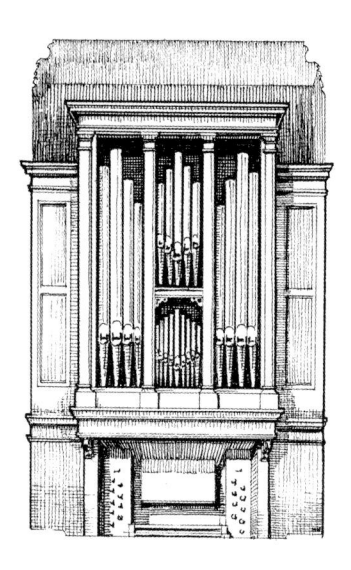

St Benet, Paul's Wharf, City of London: Herbert Norman, 1973. Organ by Hill Norman & Beard. (Drawing by Herbert Norman)

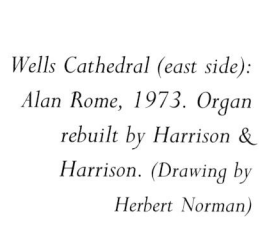

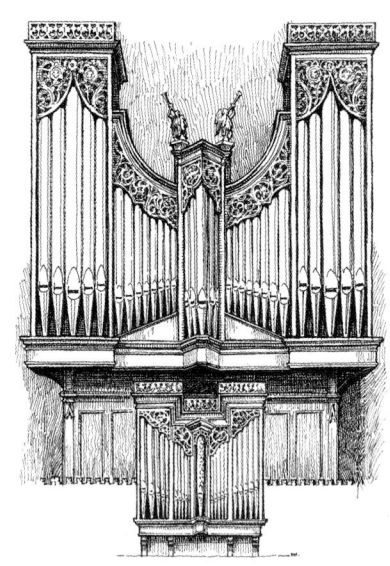

Wells Cathedral (east side): Alan Rome, 1973. Organ rebuilt by Harrison & Harrison. (Drawing by Herbert Norman)

at that time. Potter also designed the gallery on which the organ stands and a *trompe l'oeil* painting behind the organ, showing a non-existent medieval nave behind it. Sadly, the painting has since been removed to reveal a medieval window with whose design the organ case now clashes and the gallery has been spoiled by the addition of a modernist spiral staircase.

Herbert Norman moved from modernist cases, described in the last chapter, to more traditional forms for his later work. St John's Hospital Chapel, Lichfield, has a simple three-tower case with Gothic carving. The carved shoulder panels either side of the central tower conceal the swellbox containing the pipes of the upper manual.

His case at St Benet, Paul's Wharf, City of London, was an original composition, drawing on Italian ideas in that the case is essentially flat, the full pipe-lengths are exposed without pipe-shades, and the four uprights take the form of thin pilasters. The placing of the bass pipes at the sides is, however, original, as is the inversion of the centre compartment with the smaller pipes in the bottom flat.

Alan Rome, a pupil of Stephen Dykes-Bower, has designed a number of organ cases. His largest is at Wells Cathedral where, in 1973, it replaced a dull 1850s fence of bass pipes that were unworthy of their distinguished surroundings. The cresting on top of the towers is redolent of Bodley and the curved cornice to the flats is attractive. The tiny chair case is

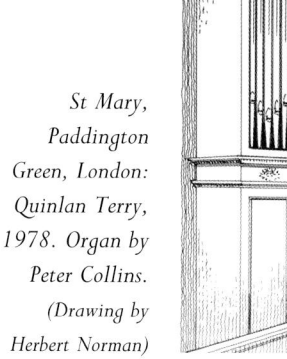

St Mary, Paddington Green, London: Quinlan Terry, 1978. Organ by Peter Collins. (Drawing by Herbert Norman)

102 The Box of Whistles

St Hugh's College Chapel, Oxford: Tamburini, Crema, 1979.

St Mary, Mold, Clwyd: Alastair Rushworth, 1973. Organ by Rushworth & Dreaper. (Drawing by Herbert Norman)

unusual in having only a single pipe in the centre tower. The big problem at Wells is that, added to an existing organ, there is no roof to the case. This means that the observer, looking up, sees through the gaps between the front pipes right up to the cathedral vault, revealing the case to be only an insubstantial screen.

Quinlan Terry is another distinguished architect who has occasionally turned his hand to organ cases. His most successful is at St Mary, Paddington Green, London. It stands on the west gallery of this late eighteenth-century church, from which Terry typically threw out all the later Victorian Gothic accretions in 1978. The case draws heavily on Georgian predecessors. For example, the curved tip-boards of the flats are a Snetzler feature and the oval upper compartments are a device used first by Harris in the early eighteenth century and continued right up to 1803 by Ohrmann and Nutt (Snetzler's successors). The ornamental urns on the tops of the towers are another eighteenth-century device, one well worth repeating.

St Hugh's College, Oxford, went to an Italian organbuilder for the 1979 organ in their chapel. The case, however, is anything but Italianate, with the whole organ (bar some bass pipes) accommodated in a chair case whose stylistic origins lie much further north. The result is a little large for the diminutive gallery on which it stands but features very delicately fretted pipe-shades hovering above the pipes in a relatively modernist manner.

The 1973 Rushworth organ in St Mary's Church, Mold, Clwyd, is unusual. Alastair

Present-day eclecticism

St Andrew and St George, Edinburgh: Christopher Gordon-Wells, 1984. Organ by Wells-Kennedy. (Photo: Christopher Gordon-Wells)

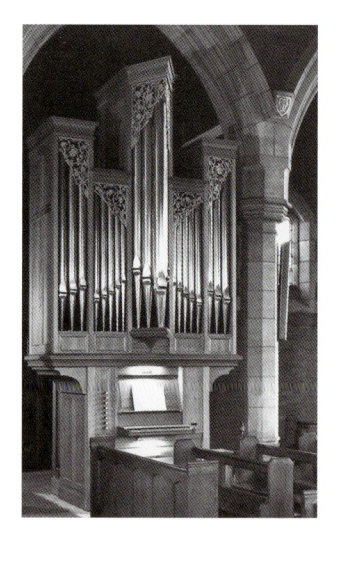

Our Lady of Good Counsel, Horsforth, West Yorkshire: David Graebe, 1982. Organ by J. W. Walker. (Photo: J. W. Walker & Sons)

Rushworth had just returned from a period working in Holland and the case exhibits the 1970s feature of some modernist cases of visible folding doors placed below the impost, as, for example, on the Collins organ at Southampton University (see page 93). At Mold this is combined with a fairly traditional style of decoration derived from the 1923 Thomas Jackson case of the previous organ at the back of the church.

The case of the organ in the Church of St Andrew and St George, Edinburgh, was also designed by the organbuilder, in this case Christopher Gordon-Wells. It is much more conservative in its overall shape than Mold but is original in many details, with pipe-shades which are neither classical, Gothic nor modernist and a central tower with an interesting bowed but flat-fronted shape and an embossed central pipe.

David Graebe has been one of our most inventive and prolific case designers. He originally worked exclusively for J. W. Walker & Sons and many of his case designs were for organs exported to America. One of his first here was for the organ in the Roman Catholic

Bolton Town Hall: David Graebe, 1985. Organ by J. W. Walker. (Photo: J. W. Walker & Sons)

Church of Our Lady of Good Counsel, Horsforth, West Yorkshire. Although the case is large and imposing, thanks to the 8 ft bass pipes in the central tower, matching the scale of the arch in which it stands, the organ behind it is quite small, having but one manual. The delicate leaf-and-stem pipe-shades are a characteristic

Graebe design and the waisted lower case adds to the elegance of the instrument.

Graebe's 1985 case for Bolton Town Hall is in quite a different style, in sympathy with its Edwardian Baroque surroundings. The central three-tower portion projects slightly and is surmounted by a curved broken pediment. The Positive division projects a little further, like a mock-chair case with a single centre tower, the whole framed within a richly carved structure surmounted by its own pediment with, on top again, three carved figures rescued from the previous organ which had been destroyed by fire. The side cases, containing the Pedal organ, have two further towers supported by caryatids, also from the previous organ.

Lancing College Chapel presented a challenge of a different kind. Here was a monumental Victorian Gothic church by R. C. Carpenter, 100 ft (30 m) from floor to ceiling. David Graebe responded with a soaring Gothic case with 16 ft front pipes and in vaguely A. G. Hill style. The special feature is, however, the intricate three-part centre tower. The horizontal trumpet pipes, sprouting from the impost in Spanish style, add power in a surprisingly unreverberant building. Graebe also designed the case of the Danish-made organ at the east

Lancing College Chapel, West Sussex: David Graebe, 1986. Organs by J. W. Walker and by Frobenius, Copenhagen.

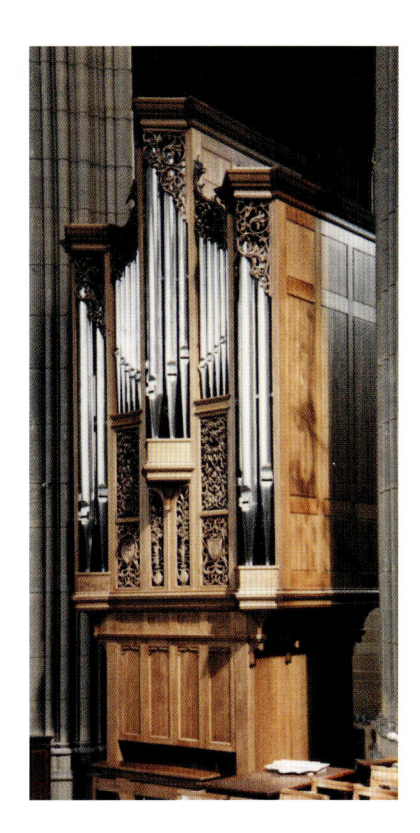

St Martin in the Fields, London: David Graebe, 1990. Organ by J. W. Walker.

end of the chapel with its intricately carved screen hiding the shutters of the swellbox of the second manual.

The 1854 case of the former organ in St Martin in the Fields, London, was a very mid-Victorian composition, at variance with James Gibbs's church of 1726. For the new organ, built in 1990, David Graebe derived inspiration from the case of the original eighteenth-century instrument built for the church by Christopher Shrider. Unlike instruments on the Continent, eighteenth-century English organs did not have Pedal keys and it was therefore necessary, in the new instrument, to expand the case sideways to accommodate the bass pipes. As a result, the imposing side towers approach the barrel-vaulted ceiling perilously closely, leaving room for a rather undersized crown and bishop's mitres. The winged cherubs on the tops of the towers are in Renatus Harris style, except that they are wearing nappies.

St Chad's Cathedral, Birmingham, is one of the few complete buildings designed by

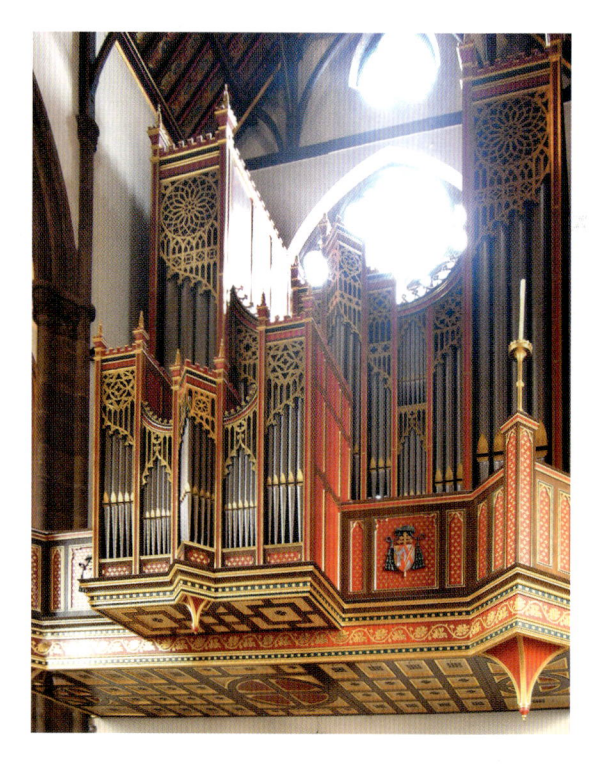

St Chad's Cathedral, Birmingham: David Graebe, 1993. Organ by J. W. Walker.

106   The Box of Whistles

A. W. N. Pugin. Although Pugin had planned an organ on a gallery under the west window, no design has survived. David Graebe responded to this situation with a design for case and gallery which drew inspiration from a known Pugin organ drawing (for a two-tower case) but went beyond it with a third (central) tower of complex form and a chair case behind the player to accommodate the Positive division of the instrument. The richness appropriate to a Pugin building was achieved by the liberal use of colour and gold. The pipe-shades, with their miniature rose windows, are a particular delight and the decoration to the underside of the chair case and gallery, so important to a case seen from below, received particular attention. Graebe was to repeat his emphasis on the appearance of the soffit of a chair case in the Nicholson organ at Christchurch Priory in 1997 (see photograph on page 5).

Stephen Bicknell is another designer who has worked for more than one organbuilder. His early work was for N. P. Mander and his 1986 adaptation of the 1898 Basil Champneys case in Mill Hill School Chapel proved to be a happy augury. The Champneys case had some excellent woodwork in the towers but there had clearly been a lack of liaison with the organbuilder and the front pipes collided with the case rather than seeming part of it. Bicknell cleverly reworked the case with new front pipes, swept cornices linking the tall centre tower with the rest of the case, plus proper end panels and a roof, the whole being supported on an arcade reminiscent

Mill Hill School Chapel: Basil Champneys, 1898, remodelled by Stephen Bicknell in 1986. Organ by N. P. Mander. (Photo: Mander Organs)

St Ignatius Loyola, New York City: Didier Grassin and Stephen Bicknell, 1992. Organ by N. P. Mander. (Photo: Mander Organs)

of the seventeenth-century Dallam case at Tewkesbury. The use of exposed tops to the front pipes under semicircular arches gives the front an Italian flavour even if the overall shape of the case is basically North European.

Although this book is largely about organ cases in the British Isles, it would be churlish to omit the impressive case of the organ in St Ignatius Loyola, New York City. Made in Britain by Mander and designed by Didier Grassin and Stephen Bicknell, it is one of the largest organ cases of its era, with 16 ft bass pipes in the side and centre towers. All the other towers, some semicircular and some of V-form, are double deck, and even the chair case has an 8 ft bass for its largest pipes. The overall style could perhaps be described as Edwardian Baroque and therefore approximately contemporary with the building that houses it.

After this exuberant exercise and his A. G. Hill/Chichester-inspired design for Chelmsford Cathedral, Stephen Bicknell designed a much more modest and restrained case for the medieval Church of All Saints, Ravensden, Bedford. It is but 5 ft 8 in (1.7 m) wide and 12 ft (3.6 m) high, with the bass of the 4 ft Principal stop as front pipes. The general design follows the model of the 1764 Byfield organ in St Mary, Rotherhithe (see page 46) which, in itself, is a simplification of the ogee-fronted cases of 20 years earlier. The simple pipe-shades derive from the work of Samuel Green in the 1780s, such as the organ built for St Thomas, Ardwick, Manchester. One cannot scale down the size of the player to match a smaller instrument so, on a small organ such as this, the console forms a bigger proportion of the front of the instrument.

All Saints, Ravensden, Bedford: Stephen Bicknell, 1997. Organ by Robert Shaftoe. (Photo: Robert Shaftoe)

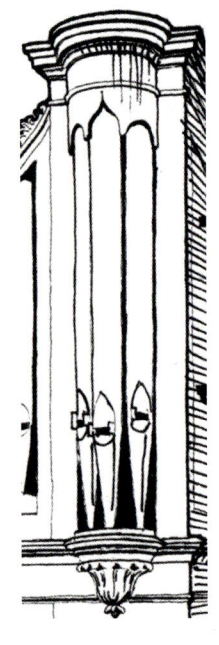

St Thomas, Ardwick, Manchester: Samuel Green, 1787. Organ now in Salford. (Detail of drawing by Herbert Norman)

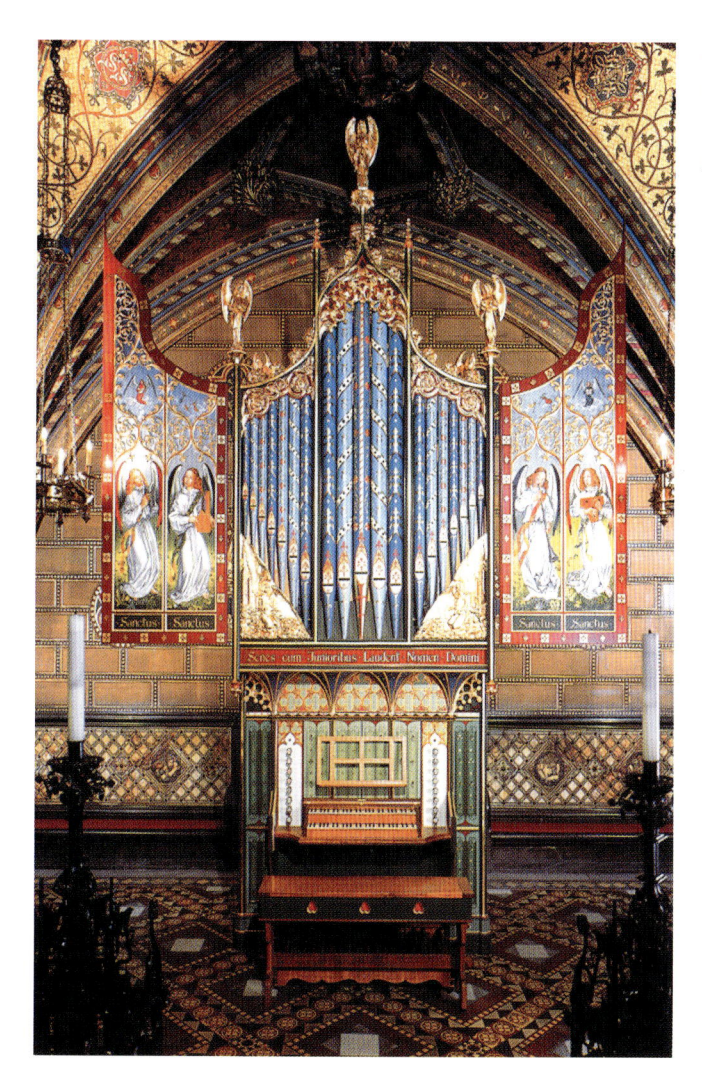

Chapel of St Mary Undercroft, Palace of Westminster: A. W. N. Pugin, 1847, realized by William Drake and John Bucknall in 1999. Organ by William Drake. (© Palace of Westminster, photo by George Garbutt)

A. W. N. Pugin woodcut. (From Sir John Sutton, A Short Account of Organs)

Another necessarily compact organ is the instrument in the Chapel of St Mary Undercroft, Palace of Westminster. This is a further example of care taken to match an organ case to the style of the building. The chapel is medieval but was lavishly furnished in Pugin style in the 1860s by E. M. Barry. Thus, although built in 1999, the case of the organ is (at the author's suggestion) a realization of a Pugin woodcut made in 1847 for Sir John Sutton's book, *A Short Account of Organs*. The colour and decoration of the front pipes is taken from that on the ribs of the vaulting. It should be noted that, to keep the case in scale with the building, the longest front pipe sounds bottom E, leaving four pipes to be placed inside. This organ is an example of an instrument where a fine case justified the organ being placed in a prominent position. The previous organ had no case and was hidden away in a position which was unsatisfactory both acoustically and musically.

A further example of a modern case based on a historic model can be found at St Wystan, Repton, Derbyshire. At the suggestion of Peter

Present-day eclecticism

St Wystan, Repton, Derbyshire: Nicholas Plumley, 1998. Organ by Peter Collins. (Photo: Peter Collins)

The oldest surviving organ case in Britain: St Stephen, Old Radnor, Powys, c.1530. (Drawing by Herbert Norman)

Collins, Nicholas Plumley used the sixteenth-century case at Old Radnor as his inspiration. The flowing and fretted pipe-shades are particularly effective but all the towers and flats are in a single plane, unlike the original, making the overall shape more two-dimensional.

Like the previous example, the 1992 instrument for the Church of St Teresa, Beaconsfield, Buckinghamshire, closely follows a historic design, in this instance going back to the eighteenth century. Roger Pulham has long had a fascination for the work of the Silbermann family of organbuilders and the design of this organ, with main and chair cases, was inspired by the organ in Ebersmunster Abbey in Alsace, even to the style of the music desk.

Of course, the organbuilder who is also a case designer, although in some ways a modern phenomenon, is merely a reversion to what was

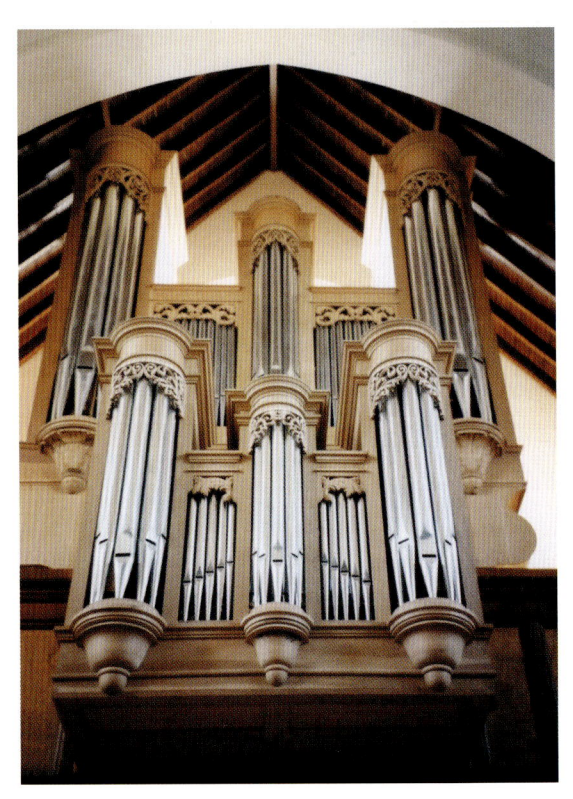

St Teresa, Beaconsfield, Buckinghamshire: Roger Pulham, 1992. Organ by Roger Pulham. (Photo: Roger Pulham)

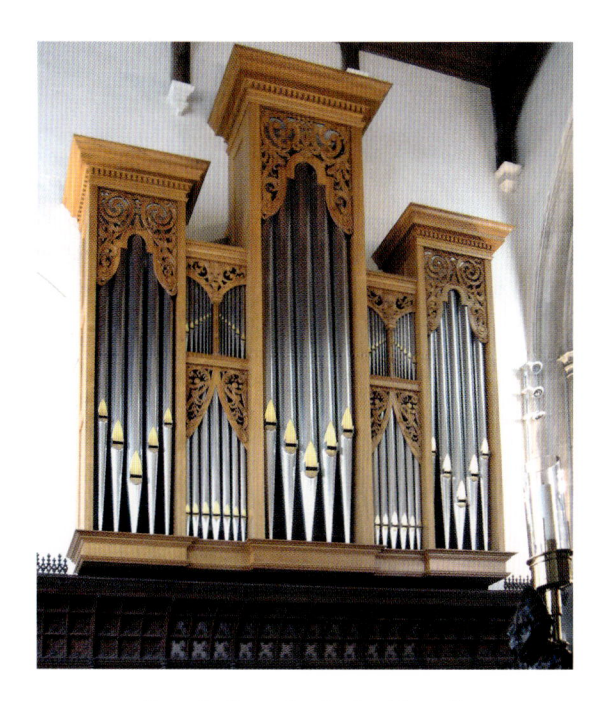

common practice up to 1820, revived in the 1880s by A. G. Hill. Kenneth Jones, based in Co. Wicklow in the Republic of Ireland, has been particularly prolific. His 1991 case in the chancel of Great St Mary, Cambridge, is typically robust and rectangular, with three broad five-pipe towers. The division of the upper storeys of the flats with central columns is original and not obviously based on any historic model.

Peter Collins is another organbuilder who produces very original designs. Although the overall silhouette of his 1989 organ in Greyfriars Kirk, Edinburgh, is very traditional North European, with its separate side towers for the Pedal division, the design is given distinction by flamboyant pipe-shades with large-scale images of animals on the angled Pedal towers.

Another instrument with a North European layout, also in Scotland, is Neil Richerby's equally rectangular instrument, on the north gallery of the Church of St Mary, Haddington,

Great St Mary, Cambridge (chancel): Kenneth Jones, 1991. Organ by Kenneth Jones.

Greyfriars Kirk, Edinburgh: Peter Collins, 1989. Organ by Peter Collins. (Photo: Peter Collins)

St Mary, Haddington, Lothian: Neil Richerby, 1990. Organ by Lammermuir. (Photo: Lammermuir Pipe Organs/Peter Backhouse)

Present-day eclecticism

St Joseph, Leicester: Neil Richerby, 2001.
Organ by Lammermuir. (Photo: Neil Richerby)

St Mary, Twickenham, Middlesex: Alan Howarth, 1995.
Organ by Harrison & Harrison.

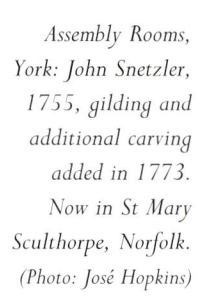

Lothian. The main case is elegantly waisted but the foliate pipe-shades form the main decorative feature.

Richerby has carried over his interest in pipe-shade design into the case of his instrument at St Joseph, Leicester. Emphasis has been added by picking out some of the decoration in gold, the lily being the symbol for St Joseph. Note also the embossed centre pipe and the gilded pipe-mouths. Interestingly, this instrument is housed in a modernist church, designed in 1967. The single central tower is reasonably common, but the triple division of the side flats is quite original. The use of small upside-down front pipes (known as 'mirror principals') is a device possibly of Dutch origin, dating back to the fifteenth century.

Assembly Rooms, York: John Snetzler, 1755, gilding and additional carving added in 1773. Now in St Mary Sculthorpe, Norfolk. (Photo: José Hopkins)

112   The Box of Whistles

The previous organ in the Georgian Church of St Mary, Twickenham, Middlesex, had a plain 'pipe-rack' front to which an ornate top cornice had been added in 1965. This was too good to lose when a new organ was made in 1995. The cornice was identified by the author as being based on that of the case of an eighteenth-century chamber organ by John Snetzler now in Sculthorpe Church, Norfolk. Alan Howarth based the detailing of the new front pipes and lower section of the case on Snetzler's original design, increased in scale to match 8 ft front pipes instead of the miniature front of the original. The case is made of softwood and painted. The pierced panels, designed and carved by Derek Riley, allow a sound outlet to the Swell division, placed in the lower part of the case. The console is terraced to keep it low and is slightly detached.

David Wood used a slightly later period as inspiration when he designed the case of the organ in the Church of St Cross, Clayton, Manchester. Although superficially it draws its style from the Gothic Revival cases of the 1820s (see, for example, Blore's case in Winchester Cathedral, page 53), the case has a solidity notably missing from the original, being three-dimensional rather than a mere screen. The other variation is that the natural lengths of the front pipes are revealed, Italian fashion, instead of being hidden behind the carving.

St Cross, Clayton, Manchester: David Wood, 1995. Organ by Wood of Huddersfield. (Based on a photograph by David Wood)

St Matthew, Sheffield: Martin Goetze, 1992. Organ by Goetze & Gwynn. (Photo: Goetze & Gwynn)

Present-day eclecticism

Collegiate Church of St Endellion, Cornwall: Martin Goetze, 2001. Organ by Goetze & Gwynn.
(Photo: Goetze & Gwynn)

St Matthew, Westminster: Didier Grassin, 1989. Organ by N. P. Mander. (Photo: Mander Organs)

Like the Lammermuir organ at Leicester, the case of the instrument in the Church of St Matthew, Sheffield shows some Dutch influences. Martin Goetze tried to imagine the sort of organ that Father Smith would have built when he first came to England from Holland after the Great Fire of London. He used as models the surviving parts of the Smith organ built for the king's private chapel at Windsor (now at Walton-on-Thames) and the instrument surviving in the Grote Kerk, Edam. The case is notable for its good proportions, even though it is actually smaller than appears, the longest pipe in the case sounding 5 ft G.

Martin Goetze used a different model for the Collegiate Church of St Endellion, Cornwall. The central three of the five pipes in the central tower form a semicircle, leading to quite a complicated cap to the tower. This feature and the semicircular arches to the flats are derived from the eighteenth-century West Country work of Renatus Harris and Brice and Richard Seede. The cow carved in the middle of the central pipe-shade is an emblem of St Endellion.

Didier Grassin's part in the huge case for the organ exported to St Ignatius Loyola, New York City has already been noted. Earlier than this, in 1989, at a time when modernist or Georgian cases were more common, Grassin designed the Gothic case of the organ in St Matthew, Westminster, London, after an idea by the late Michael Gillingham. It uses a single central tower to fit into the arch and a carved cresting to soften the outline. The embossed centre pipe and the three-sided coving above a tightly planned lower case are also particular features.

Grassin's most important work to date is the case facing into the nave of Portsmouth Cathedral. Here he has had the self-confidence, in a very prominent location, to use eclectic influences to create a very individual design. The overall massing of the case, with its solid shape, is North European and the closable doors are Gothic. The shouldered cornices to the flats and the curved tip-boards are reminiscent of the second half of the eighteenth century, yet the curved pediment and the revealed tops to the front pipes are essentially Italian in origin. The triumph of this case is the way all these diverse influences are blended into a single coherent whole. The modernist decoration on the inside of the doors is the work of Patrick Caulfield, who also designed the west doors of the cathedral.

Working on a much smaller scale (the longest pipe in the case sounds 5 ft G sharp), Didier Grassin produced an equally inventive design for

Portsmouth Cathedral (nave): Didier Grassin, 2001. Organ by Nicholson.
(Photo: Nicholson & Co./Ross Young)

Donaghadee Parish Church, Co. Down, Northern Ireland. The device of revealing the tops of the front pipes, framed in the upper part of the case without pipe-shades, is repeated. One reason for its popularity is that it avoids the cost of carving or fretting. At Donaghadee the inspiration for the case comes from the Gothic rebuilding of the church in the 1870s yet one can also detect Grassin's origins in the sharply pointed sloping roof to the instrument,

Present-day eclecticism

Donaghadee Parish Church, Co. Down, Northern Ireland: Didier Grassin, 2002. Organ by Wells-Kennedy. (Photos: David McElderry)

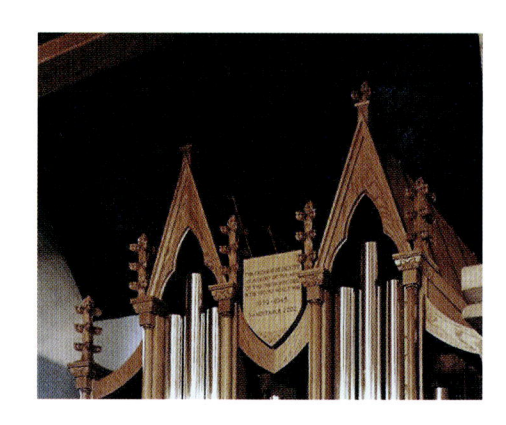

reminiscent of the nineteenth-century Cavaillé-Coll Choir organs found at the east end of French cathedrals.

The 1799 Church of St Nicholas, Gosforth, Newcastle upon Tyre, is basically classical with a low barrel-vaulted nave. The organ stands at the east end of the south aisle, constrained by a fairly narrow arch. Painted in pastel shades with gilt detailing, the cornice moulding and dentilled impost pick up ideas from elsewhere in the building. By coincidence Anthony Hall's design of 2000 uses the same Renatus Harris device of semicircular tops to the flats as the St Endellion organ described above, although the use at Gosforth of a semicircular top to a semicircular tower is unusual. The narrowness of the arch forced the tower pipes to be made over-length, leading to a loss of proportion.

Another classical church inspired a not dissimilar design in the 2001 Mander organ exported to St Peter's Episcopal Church, St Louis, Missouri. Here Aidan Nutter kept to

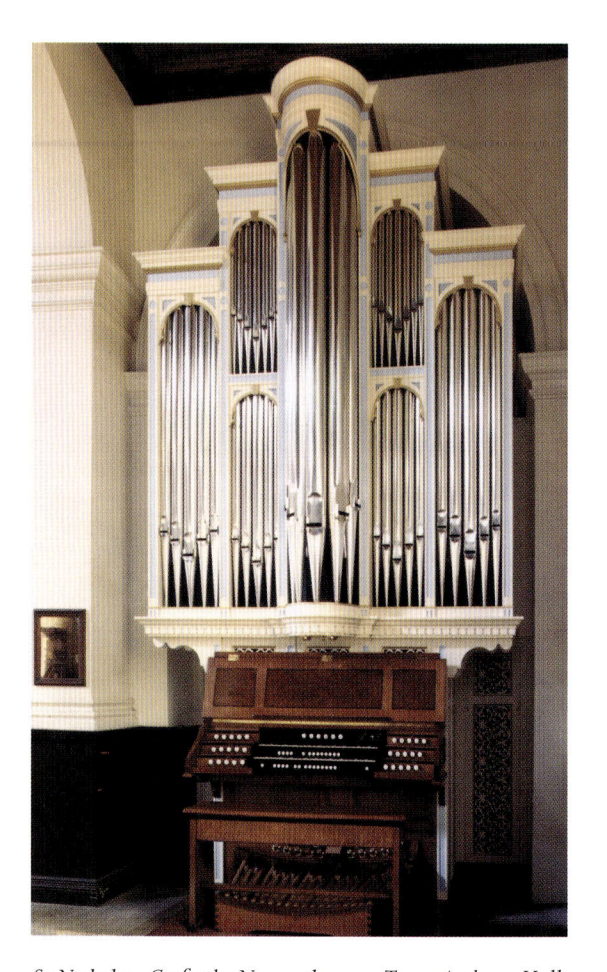

St Nicholas, Gosforth, Newcastle upon Tyne: Anthony Hall, 2000. Organ by Nicholson. (Photo: Nicholson & Co.)

116   The Box of Whistles

St Peter's Episcopal Church, St Louis, Missouri: Aidan Nutter, 2001. Organ by N. P. Mander. (Photo: Mander Organs/Bonnie Freeland)

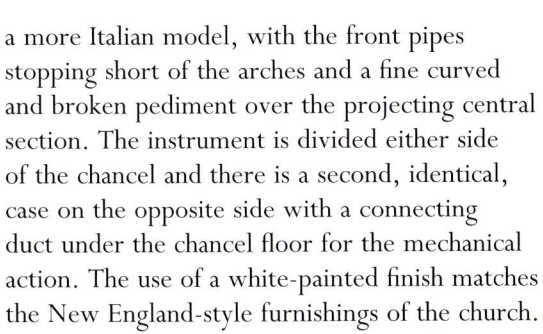

St Paul, Honiton, Devon: Kenneth Tickell, 1999. Organ by Kenneth Tickell. (Photo: Kenneth Tickell)

a more Italian model, with the front pipes stopping short of the arches and a fine curved and broken pediment over the projecting central section. The instrument is divided either side of the chancel and there is a second, identical, case on the opposite side with a connecting duct under the chancel floor for the mechanical action. The use of a white-painted finish matches the New England-style furnishings of the church.

Kenneth Tickell also used Italian-style pipe displays, framed within Roman arches, for his 1999 instrument in the Church of St Paul, Honiton, Devon. On the other hand, the overall massing and proportions of the case are North European, and the semicircular arches have not been used as an excuse to eliminate all carving. As already noted, organbuilders have recently felt the need to move away from rigid adherence to having the longest pipe in the case sounding 8 ft C. At Honiton, good proportion demanded a taller case and the biggest pipe on display, with embossed decoration, would actually sound A below bottom C if it could speak.

Kenneth Tickell's earlier case at All Saints, Oakham, Rutland (1995) clearly derives from the same general model as the Sheffield organ (see page 113), save that he used a V-plan for all three towers and a more elegant curved cornice over the flats. Derek Riley's fretted pipe-shades employ a small degree of carving to represent

Present-day eclecticism 117

All Saints, Oakham, Rutland: Kenneth Tickell, 1995. Organ by Kenneth Tickell. (Photo: Kenneth Tickell)

Worcester Cathedral: Kenneth Tickell, 2008. (Drawing by Kenneth Tickell)

intertwined oak leaves, a reference both to the material used and the name of the town. The proportions of the case were designed using the medieval *Ad Quadratum* system. However, the really original feature of this case is its location on top of a screen enclosing the entrance to the north chancel aisle chapel. The balustrade either side of the case reinforces the impression of an upper case sitting on a screen, even though the screen is actually part of the organ, housing wind supply, Pedal bass pipes and console mechanism. The balustrade is actually little more than 2 ft (0.6 m) high and, at the suggestion of Herbert Norman, the square-section spindles were turned 45 degrees to present two faces to view.

Tickell's design for the new triforium-level organ in the Quire at Worcester Cathedral, to be installed in 2008, matches the Scott furnishings with a clever elevation which derives inspiration from the work of A. G. Hill. The use of towers which return round the case sides will minimize the apparent projection from the arcade. The case incorporates the angels and carved pipe-shades from the previous cases, which were Scott's least happy work, full of dummy pipes, improbably all the same diameter.

In conclusion, the current tendency to try to match the ethos and details of the surrounding architecture is to be commended. On the other hand, we are also moving from slavish copying of traditional styles to the much more fertile field of using them as eclectic sources for truly original designs.

INDEX

Abingdon, St Helen 43
Adam, Robert, architect 46, 49
Addiscombe, Surrey, St Mildred 95
Albi, France, Cathedral 29
Aldred, Bryony, designer 9
Allen, William, organbuilder 53
Amsterdam, the Netherlands, Nieuwe Zijdskapel 14, 16
Armley, Leeds, St Bartholomew 66
Austin & Paley, architects 13

Bangor, North Wales, University, Pritchard-Jones Hall 93, 94
Baron, the Revd John 59
Bates, Theodore C., organbuilder 57
Bath Abbey: 18th c. case 38, Jackson case 77
Battle of the Organs (Smith vs Harris) 31
Beaconsfield, Buckinghamshire, St Teresa 110
von Beckerath, Rudolph, German designer & organbuilder 87
Bedford, Francis, architect 55
Berkhamsted, St Peter, Bryceson organ 7
Beverley Minster, A. G. Hill case 70
Bicknell, Stephen, designer 95, 107–8
Birmingham,
    Carrs Lane Church 89
    St Chad's Cathedral 106
    St Matthew 54
    St Philip's Cathedral 28, 42, 43
    Symphony Hall 95, 96
    Town Hall 11, 57
Bishop, James Chapman, organbuilder 55, 64
Blandford Forum, Dorset, Parish Church 48, 49
Blomfield, Sir Arthur, architect 31, 71, 72
Blore, Edward, architect 53, 54
Bodley, George Frederick, architect 70–2
Bologna, Italy, San Petronio 17, 18
Bolton, Lancashire,
    Parish Church 70
    Town Hall 104, 105
Bower, Richard, designer & organbuilder 96, 97
Bradbeer, Frank, architect & organbuilder 88, 89
Brennan, John, designer 96

Bridge, Richard, organbuilder 43, 45, 46
Brisbane Cathedral, Australia 68
Bristol,
    Cathedral 31
    Clifton Cathedral 91
    St Mary Redcliffe 81
Brustwerk (organ department placed below the impost) 6, 93, 100, 104
Bucket, Roland, artist 19
Bucknall, John, architect 109
Byfield, John, organbuilder 43, 45
Byfield, John II (son), organbuilder 46, 47

Caiger-Smith, Alan, designer 97, 98
Cambridge,
    Christ's College Chapel 36
    Clare College Chapel 87
    Emmanuel College Chapel 37
    Great St Mary: Chancel organ 111, University organ 30
    Jesus College Chapel: Harris organ 28, 'Pugin' organ 64
    Kings College Chapel 19, 20, 21, 22, 27, 28, 52
    Pembroke College Chapel 25, 26, 36
    Peterhouse Chapel 48
    Robinson College Chapel 91, 92
    St John's College Chapel 72
    Trinity College Chapel 30
Cambridge, Massachusetts, USA, Chapel of M.I.T. 84
Cardiff, Wales,
    National Museum of Wales 46
    Penarth, St Augustine 63
    Roath, St German 70, 71
Caroe, William Douglas, architect 73, 74, 78
Carpenter, Richard Cromwell, architect 65, 105
Casework: doors 2, 64, 109, false perspective 21, 23, 26, four tower 29, 52–3, 'gabled' cornice 41–4, height 4, 12, 35, straight sides 35, towers and flats 17, waisted 2, 3
Caulfield, Patrick, artist 115
Chair case 5, 22, 25, 26, 27, 32, 34, 36, 65, 88
Champneys, Basil, architect 107

Chelmsford Cathedral 108
Chichester Cathedral: Harris organ 25, 43, Hill organ 69
Christchurch Priory 5
Church, Nigel (Church & Co.), organbuilder 93
Cockerell, Christopher, architect 59
Collins, Peter, designer & organbuilder 92, 93, 94, 99, 102, 110, 111
compass of the keyboard, pre-1840, effect on case height 4
Comper, Sir Ninian, architect 12, 79
Coventry Cathedral 81, 82
Crown and Mitres, consequence of the Restoration 28, 44, 79, 80
Croydon, Surrey, St Michael 71
Cymbelstern star 79, 80, 94

Dallam, Robert (son of Thomas), organbuilder 19, 20, 22, 23
Dallam, Thomas, organbuilder 18, 19
Davis, James, organbuilder 52
Daylesford, Gloucestershire, St Peter 59, 60
Derby, St Stephen 92
Ditlevsen, Finn, Danish designer 101
Donaghadee, Co. Down, N. Ireland, Parish Church 115, 116
Douai Abbey, Berkshire 97, 98
double organ 5
Drake, William, organbuilder 45, 109
Dublin, Ireland,
    Bayside, Church of the Resurrection 91, 92
    St Mary 33
    Trinity College, Examination Hall 27
Dunster, Somerset, St George 86, 87
Durham Cathedral: Smith organ 29, Willis organ 62
Dykes-Bower, Stephen, architect 13, 68, 79, 80, 100

East-end choirs and organs – consequence of liturgical change 61–2
Edam, the Netherlands, Grote Kerk 28, 114
Edinburgh, Scotland,
    Greyfriars Kirk 111
    St Andrew & St George 104

Ely Cathedral 59, 60
England, George, organbuilder 48, 51
England, George Pyke (nephew of George), organbuilder 48–50, 53
Eton College Chapel: Hill organ 9, 67, Smith organ 30
Exeter Cathedral 26, 51, 52
Exhibition of 1851, The Great 58
van Eyck, Jan, artist 1, 2, 58, 59

Faslane, Scotland, Chapel of HMS Neptune 90
Fenham, Newcastle upon Tyne, Church of the Holy Cross 93
Finedon, Northamptonshire, Parish Church 29
Flight & Robson, organbuilders 54
Forster & Andrews, organbuilders 76
Framlingham, Suffolk, St Michael 25–6
Frant Parish Church, East Sussex 84
Frobenius, Erik, Danish designer & organbuilder 86, 91, 92, 101, 105
front pipes:
    dimensions 4, 12, 35
    dummy 12, (with two mouths 13)
    embossed 9
    false length 12, 80
    foot length 14, 27, 62, 77
    gilded 9
    materials 7, 8,
        (copper 7, 97, iron 7, plain metal 8, spotted metal 10, tin metal 8, 10, 38, zinc 8, 9, 74, 80)
    mouths 11,
        (barred/bearded 11, 12, bay-leaf 11, French 11–12, 67, gilded lips 10, mouth line 14, 62, 77, ogee 11)
    painted decoration 7, 8, 24, 26, 67
    proportions 12
Fulton, Missouri, USA, St Mary Aldermanbury, 46

Gabler, Joseph, German organbuilder 44
Geib, John, organbuilder 50, 51
Gibbons, Grinling, carver 32, 34, 35, 37
Gillingham, Michael, antiquarian 115
von Glatter-Götz, Joseph, Austrian designer and organbuilder 30, 91
Gloucester Cathedral 7, 22, 23, 24, 52
Goetze & Gwynn, organbuilders 113, 114
Goetze, Martin, designer & organbuilder 113, 114
Gordon-Wells, Christopher, designer & organbuilder 104

Gosforth, Newcastle upon Tyne, St Nicholas 116
Gothic style cases:
    evolution from 34, flamboyant 14, Gothic revival 51, medieval 14, 58, prickly Gothic 53, real Gothic revival 64
Graebe, David, architect & designer 5, 94, 104–6
Grant Degens & Bradbeer, organbuilders 88, 89
Grassin, Didier, designer 97, 99, 107, 108, 114–16
Gray & Davison, organbuilders 58, 65
Great Bardfield, Essex, St Mary 64, 65
Great Exhibition of 1851, the 58
Great Yarmouth, Norfolk, St George 45
Greek Classical style 51, 55, 56
Green, Samuel, organbuilder 47, 49, 50
Greenwich, Royal Hospital Chapel (Old Naval College) 49
Grendey, Giles, cabinetmaker 45
Griffin, Thomas, organ entrepreneur 45
Grosshartmannsdorf, Saxony, Germany, Dorfkirche 76
Guildford Cathedral 81, 84

Haddington, Lothian, St Mary 111
Hall, Anthony, designer 97, 116
Hallett, William, cabinetmaker 45
Hare, Cecil, architect 73
Harris, John (son of Renatus), organbuilder 42, 43, 45
Harris, Renatus (son of Thomas) 27, 31–3, 35, 36, 38, 40–2, 44, figure work on cases 32, 41, 42
Harris (formerly Harrison), Thomas, organbuilder 7, 23–5
Harrison, Cuthbert, designer & organbuilder 82, 85
Harrison & Harrison, organbuilders 81, 82, 85, 102, 112
Hatfield House, Hertfordshire 19
Hawkesyard Priory, Rugeley, Staffordshire 30
Hawksmoor, Nicholas, architect 37
Hemel Hempstead, Hertfordshire, Carey Baptist Church 54
Henley-on-Thames, Church of the Sacred Heart 92
Hill & Son, organbuilders 61, 62, 63, 67–70, 75
Hill, Dr Arthur G. (grandson of William) designer & organbuilder 12, 19, 63, 68–71, 75
Hill, William, organbuilder 57

Hill, Thomas (son of William), organbuilder 61
Hill Norman & Beard, organbuilders 78, 80, 84, 89, 90, 93, 101, 102
Hindley, Lancashire, St Peter 13
Holbrook, Ipswich, Royal Naval School Chapel 78
neo-Holtkamp style 83–5
Holtkamp, Walter, American designer & organbuilder 83
Honiton, Devonshire, St Paul 117
horizontal trumpets 72, 87, 94, 95
Horsforth, Yorkshire, Our Lady of Good Counsel 104
Howarth, Alan, designer 112, 113
Howell, Albert, designer 58
Hull City Hall 76
Hydraulus (Roman organ) 1

Iconoclasts, destruction of organs by viii, 22
Italian-style cases 17, 34, 117

Jackson, Sir Thomas, architect 76–7
Jardine, George, American organbuilder 83
Jenkins, Peter, architect 96, 97
Jones, Kenneth, Irish designer & organbuilder 111
Jordan, Abraham, organbuilder 38–9
Jordan, Abraham II (son), organbuilder 40, 43, 45
Jutphaas, Utrecht, Holland, Sint Nicolaas 14, 16

Kings Lynn, Norfolk, St Margaret 47
Klais, Philipp, German designer & organbuilder 95, 96
Knight, Thomas, organbuilder 47
Knopple, John, organbuilder 36

Lainson, Thomas, architect 75
Lanchester, Lucas & Lodge, architects 77–8
Lancing College Chapel, West Sussex 105
Laud, Archbishop, revival under 19
Lavant, West Sussex, St Mary 71, 72
Layout: internal 3–4, symmetrical 3
Leeds,
    Armley, St Bartholomew 66
    Town Hall (pipe materials) 7
Leicester, St Joseph 112
Lewis, Thomas C., organbuilder 81
Lichfield, Staffordshire, St John's Hospital Chapel 101, 102
Lincoln Cathedral 53
Lincoln, Henry, organbuilder 53

Penzance, Cornwall, St Mary the Virgin 52, 53
Peter Wood, organbuilder 84
Peterborough Cathedral 69, 70
Petersfield, Hampshire, Parish Church 96
Pietzsch, Siegfried, carver 94
pipe decoration (*see* front pipes, painted decoration)
pipe mouths (*see* front pipes, mouths)
pipe shades (carving to cover pipe tops) 14, 49
pipes: front (*see* front pipes), internal 3, 4
Plowman, Thomas, architect 52–3
Plumley, Nicholas, designer 99, 110
Portsmouth,
  North End, St Mark 90
  St Thomas's Cathedral: (east case) 39, (nave case) 115
position of an organ in a church 62
Potter, Robert, architect 101
Prior, Kenneth, designer 90
Pugin, Augustus Welby Northmore, architect 64, 106, 109
Pulham, Roger, architect & organbuilder 92, 93, 95, 110

Quarles, Charles, organist & dealer in organs 36

Ravensden, Bedford, All Saints 108
Reading Town Hall 75
Renaissance style 17, 33–4
Repton, Derbyshire, St Wystan 109, 110
Restoration, of the monarchy in 1660 23, 28
Richerby, Neil (Lammermuir Pipe Organs), designer & organbuilder 96, 111, 112
Richmond, Surrey, St Mary Magdalene 47
Rickmansworth, Hertfordshire, St Mary 9
Riddlesdown, Surrey, St James 78
Rieger Orgelbau, Austrian organbuilders 30, 91
Riley, Derek, carver 113, 117
Rococo, South European 44
Rollerboard 2–3
Roman organ 1
Rome, Alan, architect 77, 102
Rushworth, Alastair, organbuilder 103, 104

St Endellion, Cornwall, Collegiate Church 114
St Louis, Missouri, USA, St Peter's Episcopal 116, 117
Salford, Lancashire, St Paul 47

Salisbury Cathedral: Harris organ 42, 44, Willis organ 63
São Vicente Church, Madeira 54
Savage, James, architect 55–6
Scheemda, Groningen, Holland 9, 14, 15
Schulze, Edmund, German organbuilder 13, 66
Scott, John Oldrid (son of Sir George Gilbert), architect 72
Scott, Sir George Gilbert, architect 22, 58, 59–61
Scott, Sir Giles Gilbert (grandson), architect 72–3
Sculthorpe, Norfolk, St Mary 112, 113
Selfe, Philip H., designer & organbuilder 76, 78
Shaftoe, Robert, organbuilder 108
Sheffield, St Matthew 113, 114
Sherborne Abbey 65
Shrewsbury, St Mary 44
Shrider, Christopher, organbuilder 30, 40, 41, 106
Siena, Italy, Palazzo Pubblico 18
Silbermann, Gottfried, German organbuilder 76
Sims, Ronald, architect 95
Sion, Switzerland, Notre Dame de Valère 3, 14
Smirke, Sir Robert, architect 54–5
Smith, Bernard, organbuilder (Father Smith) vii, 11, 28–30, 35–7, 40
Smith, Christian (nephew), organbuilder 28, 37
Smith, Gerard (nephew), organbuilder 28, 29, 37
Snetzler, John, organbuilder 46, 47, 48, 112, 113
soundboard 3
South Anston, Yorkshire, St James 95
Southall, Middlesex, St George 45
Southampton, University, Turner Sims Concert Hall 93
Southwell Minster 10, 78
Spence, Sir Basil, architect 82
spires, added to earlier cases 51, 52
Stafford, St Mary 50, 51
Stamford, Lincolnshire, St John 62
Stanford-on-Avon, Northamptonshire, St Nicholas 20, 21
Strasbourg Cathedral, France 60
Street, George Edmund, architect 59, 63
Sutton, Sir John 64, 109
Sutton, the Revd F. H. (brother) 64–5
Swarbrick, Thomas, organbuilder 28, 42, 43
Sydney, Australia, Town Hall 10, 11, 75, 76

Tamburini, Giovanni, Italian organbuilder 103
Terry, Quinlan, architect 102, 103
Tewkesbury Abbey 19, 20
Thamer, Thomas, organbuilder 25, 26
Thaxted, Essex, Parish Church 53
Tickell, Kenneth, designer & organbuilder 97, 98, 117, 118
Tiverton, Devon, St Peter 37
tone cabinets 86, 89
Truro Cathedral vii, 68
Twickenham, Middlesex,
  All Hallows 10, 38
  St Mary 112, 113

Upton Scudamore Parish Church, Wiltshire 59
Urakami Cathedral, Japan 97, 99

Walker & Athron, architects 66
J. W. Walker & Sons, organbuilders 87, 88, 91, 94, 101, 104–6
Warwick, St Mary 43
Wells Cathedral 102
Wells-Kennedy Partnership, organbuilders 104, 116
Werkprinzip 6, 86, 87, 94, 100
Westhoughton, Lancashire, St Bartholomew 97
Williams Wynn, Sir Watkin 46
Willis, Henry (Father Willis) organbuilder, vii, 53, 59, 61, 62, 63, 71, 75, 77, 83
Willis, Henry III (grandson), organbuilder 72, 73
Willson, E. J., architect 53
Winchester,
  Cathedral 53–4
  College Chapel 73, 74
Windsor Castle,
  Private chapel 29
  St George's Chapel 23
Wood, David (Wood of Huddersfield), designer & organbuilder 113
Wood, Peter, organbuilder 84
Wolverhampton, St John 31
Worcester Cathedral: nave organ 99, Quire organ 118, transept case 60, 61
Wren, Sir Christopher, architect vii, 34, 35
Wymondham Abbey, Norfolk 52

York,
  Assembly Rooms 112
  Minster 54, 55
  St Martin le Grand 87
  University, Lyons Concert Hall 89

Little Stanmore, Middlesex, St Lawrence Whitchurch 37
Liverpool,
    Anglican Cathedral: chancel & crossing 73, 74, Lady Chapel 72, 73
    St George's Hall 59
Location of the organ in a church 62
London,
    City,
        All Hallows, Lombard Street 38
        Christ Church, Newgate Street 32
        City of London School 94
        Merchant Taylors' Hall 100
        St Andrew, Holborn 36
        St Andrew Undershaft 33
        St Benet, Paul's Wharf 102
        St Botolph, Aldersgate 49, 50
        St Botoph, Aldgate 41, 42
        St Bride, Fleet Street 32
        St Clement, Eastcheap 33
        St Dionis Backchurch 43
        St Edmund, Lombard Street 40
        St George, Botolph Lane 45
        St Helen, Bishopsgate 45
        St James, Garlickhythe 36
        St Katharine Cree 29
        St Magnus the Martyr, 39
        St Margaret Pattens 45
        St Martin, Ludgate Hill 57, 58
        St Mary-at-Hill 57
        St Mary Woolnoth 32
        St Mildred, Bread Street 36
        St Paul's Cathedral vii, 34–5
        St Sepulchre, Newgate Street 24, 25
        St Stephen, Walbrook 48
        St Vedast, Foster Lane 45
        Temple Church 31
    Bermondsey, St James 55, 56
    Camberwell, St Giles 58
    Clerkenwell, St James 49, 50
    Croydon, St Michael 71
    Deptford,
        St Nicholas 28
        St Paul 45
    Dulwich,
        Christ's Chapel of God's Gift 51
        St Barnabas 97, 98
    Enfield, St Andrew 45
    Hampstead Parish Church 77
    Harringay, St Paul 9, 96, 97
    Hendon, St Mary 99
    Holborn, St John's Chapel, Bedford Row 53
    Isle of Dogs, Christ Church 81
    Islington, St Mary Magdalene 53

Kensington,
    Holy Trinity, Prince Consort Road 73
    Hyde Park Chapel, Exhibition Road 84
    Royal Albert Hall 10, 83
    St Mary Abbots 40, 41
Limehouse, St Anne 58–9
Mayfair,
    Grosvenor Chapel, South Audley Street 40
    Third Church of Christ Scientist, Curzon Street 77–8
Mill Hill School Chapel 107
Notting Hill, All Saints' 80, 81
Paddington Green, St Mary 102, 103
Piccadilly, St James 32
Richmond, St Mary Magdalene 47
Rotherhithe,
    Danish Seamen's Church 86
    St Mary 46
St Marylebone,
    All Souls, Langham Place 56
    Parish Church 101
    St Peter, Vere Street 87
Shoreditch, St Leonard 43–4
South Bank, Lambeth,
    Royal Festival Hall 85
    St John, Waterloo Road 55–6
Southall, St George 45
Southwark Cathedral 71
Spitalfields, Christ Church 45
Stanmore, St Lawrence Whitchurch 37
Strand, King's College Chapel 60, 61
Tower of London, St Peter ad Vincula 30
Twickenham,
    All Hallows 10, 38
    St Mary 112, 113
Westminster,
    Abbey 68
    Palace of Westminster, Chapel of St Mary Undercroft 109
    St John, Smith Square 45, 101
    St Martin in the Fields 106
    St Matthew 114, 115
    Whitehall: Banqueting House 30, The Queen's Chapel 32
Loosemore, John, organbuilder 26
Lorimer, Sir Robert S., architect 71, 72
Lound, Suffolk, St John the Baptist 12, 79

Manchester,
    Ardwick, St Thomas 47, 108
    Clayton, St Cross 113
    Salford, St Paul 47
Martin, Sir Leslie, architect 85
Mold, Clwyd, St Mary 103

Molner, Johan, Dutch organbuilder 15
Morris, William, designer & artist 8
Muir, John, architect 87

N. P. Mander, organbuilders 95, 97, 99, 100, 107, 108, 114, 116, 117
Nash, John, architect 56
New York City, USA,
    St George's Episcopal 83
    St Ignatius Loyola 107–8
    St Paul's Chapel 51
Newcastle upon Tyne,
    Cathedral 25
    Fenham, Church of the Holy Cross 93
    Gosforth, St Nicholas 116
Nicholson & Co., organbuilders 5, 78, 97, 115, 116
Nicholson, John, organbuilder 60
Norman & Beard, organbuilders 73, 78, 79, 81
Norman, Herbert, designer & organbuilder 77, 84, 86, 87, 90, 93, 94, 101, 102
Norwich,
    Cathedral 13, 79, 80
    St Peter Mancroft 94
Nutter, Aidan, designer 116, 117

Oakham, Rutland, All Saints 10, 117, 118
Ochsenhausen, Bavaria, St George's Abbey 44
Old Radnor, Powys, St Stephen 16, 17, 110
Oxford,
    Brasenose College Chapel 76
    Christ Church Cathedral 29, 101
    Magdalen College Chapel 19, 20
    Manchester College Chapel 8
    Merton College Chapel 101
    New College Chapel 88
    Oriel College Chapel 40, 41
    Queen's College Chapel 100, 101
    St Hugh's College Chapel 103
    St Mary the Virgin 28, 40, 52, 53
    Sheldonian Theatre 76
    Wadham College Chapel 76

Pace, George, architect 87, 88
Paisley Abbey 71, 72
Palma Cathedral, Majorca 51, 52
Pearson, John Loughborough, architect 9, 53, 59, 60, 67, 68
Pease, Lancelot, organbuilder 27
pedal organ, casework 6
Penarth, Cardiff, St Augustine 63
Pennells, Andrew, designer & organbuilder 91, 92